The TV Addict's Handbook

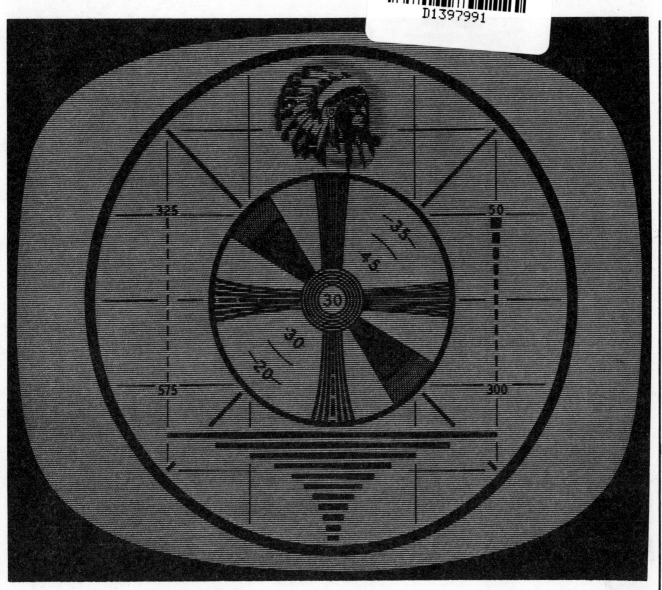

The TV Addict's Handbook

BART ANDREWS

A Dutton Paperback / E.P. DUTTON / *New York*

For
Bill Whitehead,
my favorite TV addict

Thank you, George Troiano for your photography; Howard Frank (Personality Photos, Inc., Box 50, Midwood Station, Brooklyn, N.Y. 11230; catalog available on request) for your matchless photo collection; Nancy Etheredge, a "designing" woman who has made this book much more than it really is; and, of course, Brad Dunning for everything.

Contents

PREFACE

MY FRIEND, MY TELEVISION

Like any confirmed and dedicated television addict, I take my TV watching seriously. When the set gets turned on at 7 A.M. every day (an hour later on weekends), it is done so only after intense advance deliberation. After my *TV Guide* has been read from cover to cover, I carefully check off all the programs I intend to watch for the week. This is a painstaking operation: For instance, will I watch Lucy stomp grapes (for the 177th time) on *I Love Lucy* or check in with *Adam-12* at 7 P.M.? Will it be *Today* or *Good Morning, America* at 7 A.M.? *All in the Family* or *The Munsters* rerun in the afternoon? Oh, woe is me!

A TV addict is one who enjoys television . . . a lot, a whole lot, in fact. A *real,* card-carrying TV addict might even turn down dinner with the President if his favorite show is on the same night. A TV addict is someone who takes a TV to the beach, who would take along his set on a suicide mission, who would watch a test pattern if there were nothing else on, who would rather have a TV than a bathtub (actual statistics prove that one, by the way).

For you, and for others not so fanatical, I have created *The TV Addict's Handbook,* a crazy compilation of fun, facts, and photos for media maniacs.

BART ANDREWS

Hollywood, California

TV'S FIRST STAR

The image is blurry and flawed but identifiable: Felix the Cat, hero of a thousand comic strips and a hundred animated cartoons. America's first authentic television star. Long before Ed Sullivan, long before even Milton Berle, Felix's was a name to conjure with on the two-inch tube. Beginning in the late 1920s, RCA engineers in a mid-Manhattan studio trained their arc light on a papier-mache statue of Felix, picked up the reflections on a battery of photoelectric cells and sent his likeness whizzing all the way to Kansas. There, and at points in between, it was picked up by fellow video buffs on their primitive 60-line receivers and analyzed for quality. Later, with the switch to 120-line transmission, Felix's picture improved. But despite frequent patching and repainting, by that time Felix had fallen off his turntable once too often and had to be retired in favor of a statue of Mickey Mouse. Hail and farewell, Felix.

AULD ACQUAINTANCES

Sometimes they're called sidekicks, sometimes friends, but whatever the label, they're some of our favorite acquaintances. Can you match up these famous pairs?

1. Janet Tobin _____
2. Buddy Sorrell _____
3. Sam Bolt _____
4. Duke Slater _____
5. Vivian Harmon _____
6. Jingles _____
7. Jai _____
8. Ed Norton _____
9. Michael Anthony _____
10. Henshaw _____
11. Rosie Hamicker _____
12. Barney Fife _____
13. Eddie Haskell _____
14. Porky Brockway _____
15. Cato _____
16. Trapper John McIntyre _____
17. Mr. Green Jeans _____
18. Mary Jane Lewis _____
19. Roger Healey _____
20. Sergeant Ed Brown _____

a. Ralph Kramden
b. Sally Rogers
c. Joan Stevens
d. Ernie Bilko
e. Jeff Miller
f. Wally Cleaver
g. Hawkeye Pierce
h. Tony Nelson
i. Lucille Carter
j. Tarzan
k. Gomer Pyle
l. Honey West
m. Wild Bill Hickok
n. Captain Kangaroo
o. Andy Taylor
p. Maude Findlay
q. John Beresford Tipton
r. Hazel Burke
s. Britt Reid
t. Chief Ironside

Husbands

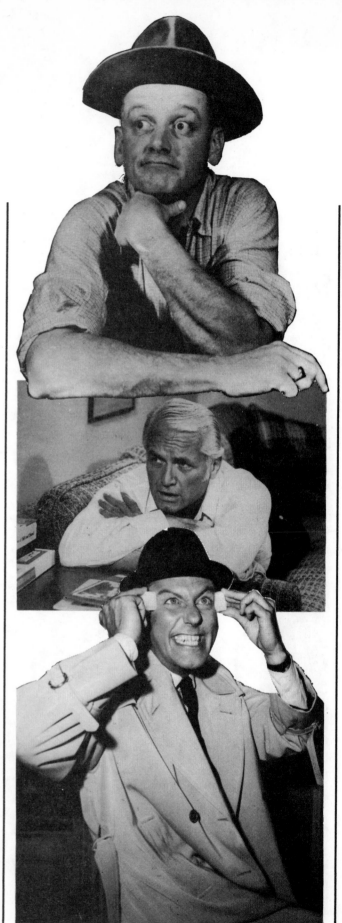

Furnish the wife's name for each husband.

1. George Jetson_____

2. Clarence Day_____

3. Chester A. Riley _____

4. Rob Petrie _____

5. Albert Arbuckle_____

6. Nick Charles _____

7. Bob Hartley _____

8. Milburn Drysdale_____

9. Ed Norton _____

10. Ted Baxter _____

11. George Baxter _____

12. Harry Morton _____

13. John Robinson _____

14. Henry Mitchell_____

15. Jerry North_____

Wives

Furnish the husband's name for each wife.

1. Margaret Anderson _____

2. Honeybee Gillis _____

3. Joan Nash _____

4. Eve Hubbard _____

5. Carol Brady _____

6. Henrietta Topper _____

7. Florida Evans _____

8. Louise Jefferson _____

9. Martha Wilson _____

10. Kate McCoy _____

11. Sally McMillan _____

12. Natalie Lane _____

13. Barbara Robinson _____

14. Donna Stone _____

15. Molly Goldberg _____

TV CONNECTIONS

Indicate the television (not personal) connection between the performers provided, i.e., they played the same role, or type of role, or they were associated on TV with the same actor or actress.

1. Herbert Anderson and Sajid Khan ____

2. Patricia Harty and Pamela Britton ____

3. Doris Day and Judy Carne ____

4. Paul Lynde and James Whitmore ____

5. Wally Cox and James Franciscus ____

6. Richard Widmark and Harpo Marx ____

7. Roger C. Carmel and Richard Deacon __

8. Ken Curtis and Dennis Weaver ____

9. Martha Rountree and Lawrence Spivak

10. Bill Cosby and Raymond Massey ____

11. Stanley Fafara and Stephen Talbot ____

12. Steve Allen and Garry Moore ____

13. Smiley Burnette and Rufe Davis ____

14. Pat Priest and Beverley Owen ____

15. Vincent Price and Otto Preminger ____

16. Bea Benaderet and Gay Hartwig ____

17. Don Knotts and Jerry Van Dyke ____

18. Paul Lynde and Arthur Hill ____

19. Anthony George and John Sylvester ____

20. Lee Bowman and Hugh Marlowe ____

My Television Photo Album

And they said Cleo was a virgin.

Sally Rogers was always good at demonstrating punch lines.

Barbara Hale and Bill Hopper worked with an ass on _Perry Mason_.

The kid couldn't even do his own trick-or-treating.

Jack Narz telling his wife why he won't be home for dinner. (That's where they got the title for the show.)

Rusty grows up. Rusty asks for a raise. Danny gets pissed.

Wouldn't it have been easier just to tell the kid that Flipper had been cancelled?

Omigod! This week's _Maude_ script has no swear words. What'll we do?

Harriet was _so_ naive.

Look who's eating cakes!

It was usually Jack Webb asking the questions, until the time his wife found out about the 18-year-old metermaid.

It ain't easy telling off a millionaire.

The latest in medical fashions. Comes with two pairs of surgical gloves.

This turkey ran twelve years.

Look who's stealing from who!

During commerical breaks, Art loved to tell his favorite jokes to the kiddies.

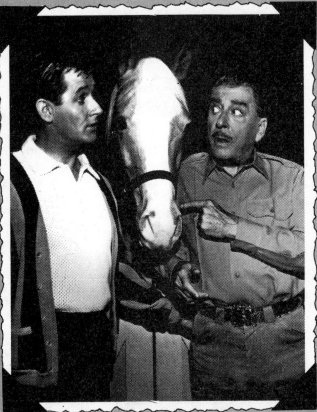

They finally found out who's getting all the funny lines.

Up, Up and Away!

Since 1951, when *The Adventures of Superman* made its television debut, "the never ending battle for truth, justice and the American way" has thrilled generations of fans. Below are twenty questions about one of the most popular adventure programs ever to reach our TV screens. Look! Up in the sky! It's a bird! It's a plane! It's a Superman trivia test!

1. Name the apartment building where Clark Kent lived.

2. What *Superman* character did John Hamilton play?

3. In what town did Clark Kent grow up?

4. What one metallic element could critically harm Superman?

5. Name the primary TV sponsor of the series.

6. Who played cub reporter Jimmy Olsen?

7. How did Superman address Lois Lane?

8. Do you recall The Man of Steel's name as a baby on planet Krypton?

9. On what 1950s sitcom did George Reeves, as Superman, make a guest appearance?

10. What actual edifice was used for the exterior shots of the *Daily Planet* Building?

11. Name Superman's parents on Earth.

12. Perry White was forever making a plea to whose ghost?

13. Inspector Bill Henderson was portrayed by what actor?

14. Complete this *Superman* opening narration: "Faster than a ———! More powerful than a ———! Able to leap ——— in a single bound!"

15. Who resided at 22 Wood Avenue, Metropolis?

16. Name the actor who played these Superman heavies: Mortimer Murray, Legs Lemmy, Si Horton, and Arnold Woodman.

17. Where did Clark Kent usually change into his Superman garb when he was in the *Daily Planet* Building?

18. Name Jimmy Olsen's aunt who lived on Moose Island off the coast of Maine.

19. What *Superman* character invented an anti-memory gas, a robot (Mr. McTavish), and a gold-making machine?

20. Name the two actresses who played Lois Lane.

The TV Guide Story

As he thumbed through the Philadelphia *Bulletin* one afternoon in 1952, publisher Walter H. Annenberg paused to ponder a full-page ad. His own morning daily, the *Inquirer*, carried no such ad and it concerned the publishing mogul. The advertisement was for a Philadelphia TV magazine called *TV Digest*, a small-size weekly that had reached a healthy circulation of 150,000. Annenberg took immediate action. For about $3 million he bought not only Philadelphia's *TV Digest* but similar magazines in Chicago *(TV Forecast)*, Washington, and New York *(TV Guide)*, added new editions of his own, and stitched them all together under the name *TV Guide*.

Thus, on April 3, 1953, was born the tiniest weekly bargain on any newsstand (its pages were 2½ square inches smaller than *Reader's Digest*). It sold for 15¢.

TV Guide has grown from its initial ten editions and a 1,500,000 circulation to eighty-nine editions and a weekly circulation in excess of twenty million, making it the largest weekly magazine in the world. This blanket coverage gives *TV Guide* what amounts to an impregnable monopoly. The magazine smothers the United States and part of Canada, with editions varying from a high of 2,660,000 (metropolitan New York) to a low of 40,000 (Montana).

When *TV Guide* made its bow in 1953, some 24 million set-owning families were watching Milton Berle, Arthur Godfrey, Ed Murrow, Jackie Gleason, *Studio One, Dragnet,* and a television classic, *I Love Lucy.* Lucille Ball and her real-life, infant son, Desiderio Alberto Arnaz IV—better known as Desi, Jr. —appeared on the first cover of the brand new television magazine.

Desi, Jr.'s birth was a headline affair. Newspapers put it on the front page, and when Lucy's television son, Little Ricky, was born the same day, January 19, 1953, the show garnered the largest rating in TV history. Naturally, all the major magazines wanted exclusive pictures of "the $50,000,000 baby" for their covers. In fact, the pictures had already been promised to *Life* and *Look.* At least that is what Desi Arnaz told a *TV Guide* representative at a meeting a few weeks after the birth. The pictures had been taken at the Arnaz ranch in Northridge and were at that moment in Desi's desk drawer.

At one point during the meeting Desi suddenly rose from his chair and pushed the stack of covered photos toward his visitor. Then he excused himself to go to the men's room, making it clear that if several pictures were missing when he got back, he would not notice.

As Dwight Whitney, the astute West Coast editor of *TV Guide,* says, "It was an impulsive and generous gesture . . . also a symbolic one. Lucy, the medium and the magazine, as it were, grew up together, she to dominate and strongly influence TV comedy for the next two decades, television to be transmuted from electronic plaything to powerful communications force, and *TV Guide* to record it."

Just behind the cover of the first issue appeared an introductory editorial that said, in part: "Your magazine is dedicated to serving constructively the television

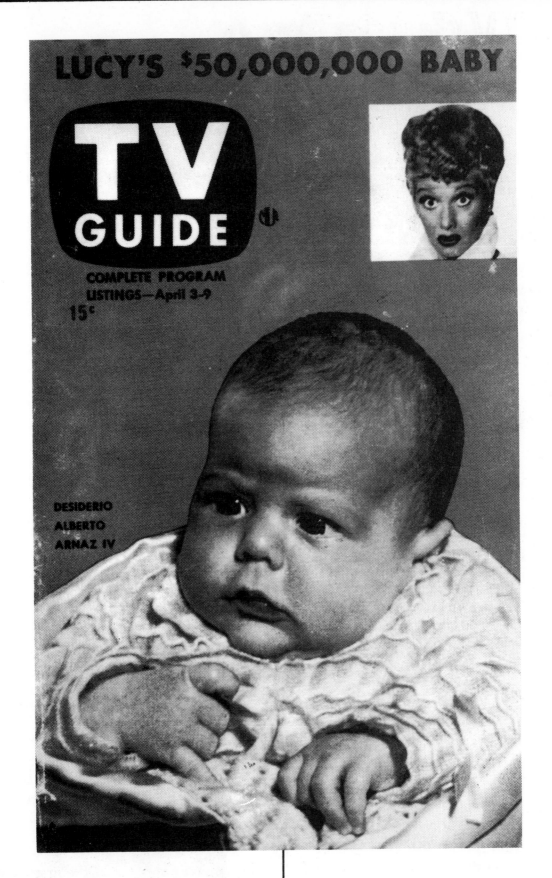

LUCY'S $50,000,000 BABY

TV GUIDE

COMPLETE PROGRAM
LISTINGS—April 3-9

15¢

DESIDERIO
ALBERTO
ARNAZ IV

viewer.'' Although twenty-five years have
passed, that goal has not changed, just the
price (35¢).

WHO SAID IT?

Can you identify the personalities who were famous for the following quotations?

1. "Put a little fun in your life—try dancing!"

2. "One of these days, . . . one of these days—POW! Right in the kisser!"

3. "I don't mess around, boy."

4. "What a revoltin' development *this* is!"

5. "Well, I'll be a dirty bird!"

6. "Abracadabra, please and thank you."

7. "Good night and God bless."

8. "I arrest you in the name of the Crown."

9. "Will it be a hit or a miss?"

10. "Hi-ho, Steverino!"

11. "I'd like you to meet my brother George."

12. "So long and be good to yourself."

13. "Would *you* like to be Queen for a Day?"

14. "Heck, no!"

WHO SAID IT?

15. "Sorry about that."
_____

16. "Is it bigger than a breadbox?"
_____

17. _"¡Miraquetienecosalamujeresta!"_
_____

18. "Good night and a good tomorrow."
_____

19. "Peace."
_____

20. "Don't fight it—it's bigger than both of us."
_____

20

Could You Have Hit the Jackpot?

Before *The $64,000 Question* made its debut on CBS in June of 1955, there were a passel of other quiz programs on the air. In fact, these brainteaser broadcasts had already given away about $10 million in cash and merchandise by the time actor Hal March became the big-money quizmaster.

Many of us have often had the feeling we could have hit the jackpot "if we were only up there." To put this assumption to the acid test, try your luck (and intelligence) on twenty-five of the highest-paying jackpot sticklers of all time.

Had you answered all of them correctly, you could have cashed in to the tune of over $150,000 (before taxes). Add up your score in terms of dollars won and don't declare a cent of it to Uncle Sam.

1. How many amendments are there to the Constitution? (*You Bet Your Life*—worth $5,000.)

2. You are climbing the famous Atlas Mountains. Name the continent you're on. (*Strike It Rich*— $500.)

3. What was the name of the B-50 plane which made the first non-stop flight around the globe in the spring of 1949? (*Break the Bank*— $8,870.)

4. What was the exact number of human beings on the Ark during the 40-day deluge? (*The Big Payoff*— mink coat, complete woman's wardrobe, trip for two anyplace in the world: approximately $6,000.)

5. Who was the French sculptor who created "The Thinker"? (*You Bet Your Life*— $2,000.)

6. In what year did Lincoln deliver his Gettysburg Address? (*On Your Account*— $4,500.)

7. *"No stranger I to diamonds,*
I've won a hero's crown,
Think of several Bills and you'll find me,
Now my tackle is winning renown."
Who am I? (*Feather Your Nest*— $2,500 worth of furniture.)

8. In 15 seconds: a. The first contestant will select a two-figure number, the other will subtract one digit from the other. As many as possible. b. Name as many occupations as you can that require a ladder. c. Give as many words as possible that end in "th." (*Two For the Money*— $6,375.)

9. The real story of a man named Matt Cvetic was made into a movie. It told how he risked death and suffered humiliation for his country. Name the movie. (*Break the Bank* — $11,840.)

10. On May 28, 1934, the Dionne Quintuplets were born near a little town in Ontario, Canada. What town? (*You Bet Your Life*— $1,500.)

Could You Have Hit the Jackpot?

11. *"In the State of Ohio on the very top,*
    My trio and I made it first,
    With Robin I'm sharing, 'bout shapes I was
    caring,
    My boys thought the ride was the worst."
    Who am I? (*Feather Your Nest*— a $1,500 living room suite.)

12. Name the United States President who made "White House" the official name of the executive mansion. (*The Big Payoff*— $6,000.)

13. There's a time in the title of a famous movie of 1950 which starred Gregory Peck as an air-base commander in England, determined to win the war at all costs. What is the title? (*Strike It Rich*— $500.)

14. "La Gioconda" is the original name for one of the most famous paintings in the world. What is the popular name? (*You Bet Your Life*— $1,500.)

15. The Brooklyn Dodgers and the Boston Braves once battled for 26 innings, the longest game in modern major league baseball. It ended in a 1–1 tie. Two starting pitchers went the whole 26 innings. Who were they? (*Break the Bank*— $9,900.)

16. What is the name of Shakespeare's famous clown in his plays, *Henry IV* and *The Merry Wives of Windsor*? (*Strike It Rich*— $500.)

17. In 15 seconds: a. Give as many girls' names as possible beginning with letters "A, B, and C," b. Name as many animals as possible who normally climb trees, c. Name as many living heavyweight boxing champions as you can. (*Two for the Money*— $4,200.)

18. William H. Bonney was shot and killed by Sheriff Pat Garrett. Who was Bonney? (*You Bet Your Life*— $6,000.)

19. Name the war fought by the United States between 1802 and 1805 over payment of tribute. (*The Big Payoff*— $6,000.)

20. *"I was a little fighter,*
Two islands are part of my fame,
My code couldn't be righter,
Rip Van Winkle took part of my name."
Who am I? (*Feather Your Nest*— $1,350.)

21. An ancient country in Europe is south and west of the Rhine, west of the Alps and north of the Pyrennes. The Celts were among its chief inhabitants. What's the name of this ancient country? (*The Big Payoff*— $10,000 in trips and merchandise.)

22. What was the food of the gods on Mt. Olympus that insured them strength, power, beauty, and immortality? (*You Bet Your Life*— $6,500.)

23. There's a time in the title of a popular play by William Saroyan. It is about people in a San Francisco waterfront tavern who philosophize about life. It was awarded the Pulitzer Prize in 1940 but the author refused it. What is the title? (*Strike It Rich*— $500.)

24 & 25. Now you're on your honor. Would you recognize the tunes, "The Navy and the Army, the Army and the Navy" and "The Girl in the Blue Dress"? If your answer is yes, you would have picked up $35,250 and $22,400 respectively on *Stop the Music*.

The Best of Nielsen

Ratings represent a matter of life or death on the air to virtually every television star and series. As the only method of determining quickly the size of each program's audience, ratings decide whether a show continues or is cancelled.

The Nielsen ratings, reported by the A.C. Nielsen Company of Chicago, are based on TV usage in 1200 sample households spread across the country. The sample ensures that the households are distributed nationally, as is our population, and that the composition of the sample (age, sex, family size, income, etc.) very closely reflect those of the entire population.

An electronic device hooked to the TV sets in the 1200 households and connected by special telephone lines feed information into the giant Nielsen computer located in Dunedin, Florida. It records minute-by-minute the tuning activity of all operable TV sets in the household—whether the sets are on or off, and what channel is being tuned in and when. These results are then extended, or projected, to the entire U.S. population.

The following compilation of twenty-eight years of television represents Nielsen's finest— the top-rated TV shows of every year. You might be surprised!

1951–52 ARTHUR GODFREY'S TALENT SCOUTS
This professional "amateur show" debuts December 6, 1948, and is followed by Godfrey's other CBS show, *Arthur Godfrey and His Friends,* giving the star two simultaneous prime-time programs.

1950–51 TEXACO STAR THEATRE
"Mr. Television," Milton Berle, begins his NBC video vaudeville show on June 8, 1948. It features Arnold Stang, Ruth Gilbert, Sid Stone, and the four Men from Texaco who sing the show's opening theme. For years, Tuesday night belonged to Berle, and he is credited with "selling" more TV sets than anyone else.

1952–53 I LOVE LUCY
The Lucille Ball-Desi Arnaz situation comedy premieres October 15, 1951, on CBS and officially becomes the Number One show on April 7, 1952, with the episode "The Marriage License." Little Ricky is born this season and the episode garners a phenomenal 71.7 Nielsen.

1953–54 I LOVE LUCY
Lucy, Ricky, Fred, and Ethel continue their slapstick hijinx for a third year. It is the season when Lucy falls in a starch vat, goes on TV to sell Aunt Martha's Old-Fashioned Salad Dressing, plays her own version of golf, and invites Tennessee Ernie Ford to spend a few weeks at the Ricardos' apartment.

1955–56 THE $64,000 QUESTION
Quizmaster Hal March introduces the "isolation booth" on June 7, 1955, on CBS, courtesy of Revlon. Contestants include Gino Prato on opera, Dr. Joyce Brothers on boxing, and Vincent Price on art. The show folds on November 2, 1958, amidst the infamous quiz show scandals.

1954–55 I LOVE LUCY
With Vivian Vance as Ethel Mertz and William Frawley as her husband Fred, the Ricardos head for Hollywood so Ricky can make *Don Juan.* There Lucy tangles with the likes of William Holden, Hedda Hopper, Richard Widmark, Van Johnson, and John Wayne whose footprints she steals from Grauman's Chinese Theatre.

1956–57 I LOVE LUCY
For its sixth and last season, *Lucy* adds six-year-old Richard Keith to the cast as Little Ricky, Lucy gets a loving cup stuck on her head, works in a pizzeria, dresses up like Superman, and tangles with Bob Hope. The Ricardos and Mertzes also move to Westport, Connecticut, before the show ends its run on May 6, 1957.

1957–58 GUNSMOKE

In its third season on CBS, this "adult" western, which debuted September 10, 1955, features 6'5" James Arness as Marshal Matt Dillon, Amanda Blake as Miss Kitty Russell, Dennis Weaver as the lame deputy, Chester Goode, and Milburn Stone as Doc Galen Adams.

1958–59 GUNSMOKE

The Dodge City western, originally introduced to television by John Wayne (he was offered the Dillon role but turned it down), is still only a half-hour show. In that first episode of 1955, "Matt Gets It," Dillon is gunned down by a vicious Texan, but manages to recover in thirty minutes.

1959–60 GUNSMOKE

Now in its fifth year, this western begins each week with a shot of Dillon on horseback delivering a short sermon at a hilltop cemetery. "On Saturday night in Dodge City, too many men think they'll find courage at the bottom of a whiskey bottle. I know, because I'm the United States Marshal—Matt Dillon."

1960–61 GUNSMOKE

This is the last season for the half-hour show, as it will change over to a full hour the following season and remain that way until its cancellation after the 1974–75 season. It will remain a popular show for many years, grabbing the number two spot for the 1969–70 season.

1961–62 WAGON TRAIN

A series that debuted September 18, 1957 on NBC hits the top spot on the Nielsen charts in its fifth season, although it was the second most popular show for the previous three years. Ward Bond plays Seth Adams, and young Robert Horton plays scout Flint McCullough.

1962–63 THE BEVERLY HILLBILLIES
Assailed by critics, this bucolic sitcom premieres September 26, 1962, on CBS and is an instant hit. It stars Buddy Ebsen as Jed Clampett, Irene Ryan as Granny, Donna Douglas as Elly May, and Max Baer, Jr. as Jethro.

1965–66 BONANZA
Starring Lorne Greene as Ben Cartwright and Dan Blocker as son Hoss and Michael Landon as Little Joe, the series continues its lead even without Pernell Roberts.

1963–64 THE BEVERLY HILLBILLIES
In its second year, Jed, Granny, Elly May and Jethro continue their exalted position in the ratings. Created by Paul Henning, the series will remain on the air nine seasons and make millions in syndication.

1966–67 BONANZA
For the third year in a row, the Ponderosa is the setting for the top-rated program, airing Sundays at 9 P.M. It will remain a weekend western staple until midway through the 1972–73 season.

1964–65 BONANZA
This western, which premiered September 12, 1959, on NBC and is in its sixth semester, manages to move up the charts to the Number One slot after a few years in second and third position. Pernell Roberts, who played Cartwright son Adam, leaves this year.

1967–68 THE ANDY GRIFFITH SHOW
The series which debuted October 3, 1960, on CBS as a spin-off of *The Danny Thomas Show,* stars Griffith as Sheriff Andy Taylor of Mayberry, North Carolina; Ronny Howard as his son Opie; and Don Knotts as Deputy Barney Fife. This is its last season before reverting to a "spin-off" titled *Mayberry, R.F.D.*

1968–69 ROWAN AND MARTIN'S LAUGH-IN

This NBC satirical revue premieres January 22, 1968, as a midseason replacement for the ailing *Man From U.N.C.L.E.* An immediate hit, the program features outrageous comedy sketches, offbeat one-liners, and song parodies performed by Goldie Hawn, Judy Carne, Alan Sues, and Lily Tomlin.

1969–70 ROWAN AND MARTIN'S LAUGH-IN

From "beautiful downtown Burbank," *Laugh-In* continues to garner immense ratings under the direction of producer George Schlatter. Regular segments of the show include "The Fickle Finger of Fate" award and courtroom sketches called "Here Come the Judge." It will remain on-the-air through the 1972–73 season.

1970–71 MARCUS WELBY, M.D.

In its second season, the Robert Young-starring medical drama, which debuted on ABC September 23, 1969, features heartwarming stories about Welby and his young assistant, Dr. Steve Kiley played by James Brolin. It runs seven years.

1971–72 ALL IN THE FAMILY

Norman Lear takes a British TV sitcom, *Till Death Us Do Part,* changes its setting and characters, and CBS reluctantly puts it on the air as a midseason replacement for *The Governor and J.J.* on January 12, 1971.

1972–73 ALL IN THE FAMILY

In their second full season, the Bunkers—Archie (Carroll O'Connor), Edith (Jean Stapleton), and their daughter Gloria (Sally Struthers) and son-in-law Mike Stivic (Rob Reiner)—lead the Nielsen parade again.

1973–74 ALL IN THE FAMILY

CBS makes a number of time-slot changes, finally settling on Saturday night where the series gains an ever-increasing audience. Archie Bunkerisms like "meathead," "dingbat," and "stifle yourself" become part of the American lexicon. The show also manages to spawn *Maude, Good Times,* and *The Jeffersons.*

1974–75 ALL IN THE FAMILY

For the fourth time, Lear's brash brainchild hits the top Nielsen spot, and Lear's other offspring, *Sanford and Son,* is the second most popular series. The Stivics move out of 704 Houser Street and into George and Louise Jefferson's house next door.

1975–76 ALL IN THE FAMILY

Mike and Gloria have a son, Joey, as the series stays on top of the heap. Writers will explore some controversial issues like menopause, rape, infidelity, impotence, and Nixon. Edith goes to work as a volunteer helper at the Sunshine Home, a rest house for senior citizens.

1976–77 HAPPY DAYS

In its third season, this nostalgic sitcom, which debuted January 15, 1974, on ABC stars Ron Howard as Richie Cunningham, Milwaukee high school student, and Henry Winkler as Arthur Fonzarelli who becomes better known as "The Fonz."

1977–78 LAVERNE & SHIRLEY

Premiering January 27, 1976, this spin-off of *Happy Days* features Penny Marshall as Laverne DeFazio and Cindy Williams as Shirley Feeney, bottle-cappers at the fictional Shotz Brewery in Milwaukee. The show is likened by critics to the old *I Love Lucy* show with Laverne and Shirley being Lucy and Ethel.

The Lucille Ball Puzzle

Hidden among the maze of letters are the answers to the thirty-eight Lucy clues provided. To locate them, simply read forward, backward, up, down, and diagonally. You must always travel in a straight line, and you cannot skip letters. Draw a circle around each answer that you discover. Letters are permitted to be used more than once, and words may overlap. You will not use all the letters in the maze. Good luck, Lucy lovers!

1. Sr. and Jr. _____

2. Miss Vance _____

3. Lucy's lady scribe _____

4. Fred's spouse _____

5. Lucy's last TV series _____

6. Mr. Holden _____

7. He played Fred Mertz _____

8. Mrs. Gary Morton _____

9. Craig's sister _____

10. He owned the Unique Employment Agency _____

11. Mr. Ricardo _____

12. Mary——Croft _____

13. 623——68th Street _____

14. Lucy and Ethel filled a giant freezer with it _____

15. Miss Arden _____

16. She played Caroline Appleby _____

17. The Arnazes' production company ——

18. Sherman——, Viv's son _____

19. Mr. Oppenheimer _____

20. "I Love Lucy" director _____

21. Miss Ball's recent movie musical ——

22. Mr. Conreid _____

23. One of Ricky's favorite songs _____

24. Mr. Gordon _____

25. Little Ricky to Lucy _____

26. She played Lucy Carter's daughter ——

27. He played Mr. Barnsdahl, a banker ——

28. Lucy's second series, "The——" ——

29. Ricky's Hollywood movie _____

30. Miss Ball co-starred with him in *Fancy Pants* and *Sorrowful Jones* _____

31. She played Lucy's mother _____

32. This Marx Brother appeared on "I Love Lucy" _____

33. Mr. Schary _____

34. This company published "I Love Lucy" comic books _____

```
H S N A H O Y E L G A B
E L A G M D R A C E L I
Y C U L S E R E H E B L
K P J C P S A A H A E L
C D N O I I H T B S N F
I H O P E L E A R T A R
R C D R Y U L N I V L A
I R O A I U C E I J K W
S I R H C S N V B I L L
E S E I U O U E M A M E
D L E I F N A D E L L Y
E N A J W O H S Y C U L
```

35. Where Lucy Carmichael first lived _____

36. Candy Moore played her _____

37. "My Favorite Husband," George———

38. Phoebe Littlefield's nightclub-owner hubby _____

PRIVATE I's

I...

1. . . . was the one-armed Chief Inspector for Scotland Yard.

2. . . . was Peter Gunn's girlfriend and sing at Mother's nightclub.

3. . . . played Boston Blackie.

4. . . . am Lloyd Nolan, one of the actors who portrayed this hero.

5. . . . was a millionaire police captain on the Metropolitan Homicide Squad.

6. . . . portrayed the intrepid McGraw.

7. . . . assisted Tracy Steele when not singing at the Hawaiian Village Hotel.

8. . . . was a private investigator who gathered information for Perry Mason.

9. . . . kept a wild cat as a house pet.

10. . . . assisted my partner who wore badge number 714 of the Los Angeles Police Department.

11. . . . played Bill Weigand on *Mr. and Mrs. North*.

12. . . . was a former private eye who became mystery editor for a publishing house.

13. . . . played Matt Grebb, detective with the San Francisco Police Department.

14. . . . have starred in many TV series, but my first was one based on a Mickey Spillane character.

15. . . . was played by Lee Bowman, Hugh Marlowe, Jim Hutton, and Lee Philips.

Howdy with his mentor, Buffalo Bob.

"The President of All the Boys and Girls"

Jeff Judson, Jr. with Bart Andrews

Many consider it the most popular children's television show ever; a classic, a true pioneer in those early days of six-inch screens and test patterns. Spanning three decades, Howdy Doody managed to show his multi-freckled face 2,543 times on NBC, certainly a tribute to his overwhelming popularity. But, despite its Peabody Award "for distinguished programming," to others, the show was just another loud, commercial program. Well, yes, it *was* loud, and maybe it *was* too commercial, but it was spontaneous, unpredictable, and, best of all, "live." It boasted few special effects, no taping, no big budgets, just a small, dedicated group of talented people who managed against all odds to create a successful program for a crude, new medium television.

Like most early TV, *Howdy Doody* had its origins in radio. Bob Smith, the adult host and voice of Howdy, had his own radio show in New York during the forties, *The*

Triple-B Ranch, a western quiz show for kids. One of his characters was Elmer, a grubby Gabby Hayes-type who usually greeted everyone with a boisterous "Howdy Doody." Then along came Martin Stone, producer of TV's *Author Meets the Critics,* who was challenged by NBC to get together a children's show. Stone knew Buffalo Bob (he's from Buffalo, New York), and the two created *Puppet Playhouse,* whose name was soon changed to *Howdy Doody.* The program started out with a four-man production crew, ten technicians, and a $600 budget (Smith was paid $100) on December 27, 1947.

The Elmer character of radio was used for only a short time on TV. In addition to contract problems with its creator, Frank Paris, the original Howdy marionette was thought to be too ugly and too scary for a young audience, so a month or so later, a new image was created (by the folks at Disney), the one we *Howdy Doody* fans will long cherish—red hair, freckles (72 of them), sleepy-eyes, stuck-out ears, and wearing a plaid shirt and cowboy boots. (Actually, there were three Howdy marionettes: the one seen on the show in close-ups, a duplicate used for long shots named Double Doody, and a stringless doll used for still photography called Photo

This Howdy Doody marionette was one of the countless items sold during the fifties. It was manufactured by Peter Puppet Playthings of New York, and featured "unitrol."

Doody. Howdy also had an adopted sister, Heidi!)

The program featured more than merely Howdy and Buffalo Bob. There were dozens of other characters, some of them human, some puppet. Because Doodyville, U.S.A. (the setting for *Howdy Doody*) was a circus town, it was populated by circus folk. And what's a circus without a clown? Remember the clown who never spoke, who was always pulling pranks, who carried a seltzer bottle? Clarabell Hornblow Clown was his name. Originally played by Bob Keeshan (TV's Captain Kangaroo) whose job it had been on the show to hold up cue cards, Clarabell was mute for two very good reasons. Keeshan had never acted before a camera, and, more importantly, it was cheaper to hire an actor for a nonspeaking role (Smith was budget-conscious). Only once was Clarabell's silence broken, on that last show, September 30, 1960, when Lew Anderson (who had inherited the clown job from Bobby Nicholson who played it after Keeshan left the cast) said, "Goodbye, kids."

Dayton Allen, a talented performer who later became famous for the phrase "Why not?" on Steve Allen's show, was the voice of many characters: Mr. Phineas T. Bluster, mayor of Doodyville; John J. Fadoozle, America's Number One Private Eye; Ugly Sam, the weight-lifting wrestler; Sir Archibald, the Safari leader; Flub-A-Dub, that generic misfit animal; Pierre the chef; and a few others.

One character who quickly graduated from puppet status to person was Princess

"The President of All the Boys and Girls"

Howdy, Buffalo Bob, and an unidentified female admirer.

Summerfall Winterspring. Played by a former Broadway singer, Judy Tyler, the Tinka-Tonka princess was one of the few females seen on the show (except, of course, for the little girls who comprised part of the Peanut Gallery). Another well-known live character was the sour-pussed Chief Thunderthud, played by Bill LeCornec who also portrayed Oil Well Willy and Dr. Singsong, and was the voice of Dilly Dally. The Ooragnak (Kangaroo spelled backwards) Tribe leader is best remembered for his "Kowa Bonga" outbursts.

Flub-Dub, later named Flub-A-Dub because it was easier to pronounce, was that cockamamie creature who had a cocker spaniel's ears, a duck's bill, a cat's whiskers, a giraffe's neck, a pig's tail, a seal's flippers, a dachshund's body, and the memory of an elephant. And he loved to eat meatballs!

Dilly Dally, as the name suggests, was the lazy, put-it-off-till-tomorrow, bespectacled puppet often seen with a mop but who seldom used it. Of course, there was Captain Windy Scuttlebutt, Hefflesniffer Booglegut, Mambo the elephant, Tizzy the dinosaur, the Bloop, Hyde and Zeke, and Howdy's pet dog, Windy.

One of the most famous of all *Howdy Doody* characters was Phineas T. Bluster. One of triplets (Hector Hamhock Bluster and Don Jose Bluster were his brothers), Bluster was the cantankerous mayor of Doodyville who constantly tried to prove his popularity, but caused more trouble than anything else. Phineas was a schemer, and grumpy and crafty and stingy, an

Howdy Doody and Mr. Bluster celebrate Thanksgiving in Doodyville, 1956.

all-around mean old man. Jealous, he once tried to start his own TV show, *Howdy Bluster*. (Can you imagine?)

Behind-the-scenes was songwriter Edward Kean who wrote the show from 1947 to 1955. Besides scripts, Kean was responsible for the many tie-in books and records that proliferated during the 1950s. Kean also contributed to the radio and Canadian versions of *Howdy Doody* (the Canadian edition featured Timber Tom as host, played by Robert Goulet). Rufus Rose and Rhoda Mann handled most of the marionettes, and Milt Neal created the artwork for the show as well as for the merchandising spin-offs.

During that era, some 600 companies applied for the right to manufacture Howdy Doody paraphernalia of almost every description. Those crayon sets, puzzles, Royal Gelatin box trading cards, Howdy Doody bandaids, clothing, dolls, puppets, jewelry, games, and books of the 1950's are now prized pieces in nostalgia collectors' closets.

When the show's budget got out of hand and Buffalo Bob's health was on the wane, NBC decided to cancel the legendary show. Also, several of *Howdy*'s best sponsors, Wonder Bread, Hostess (Twinkees), Kellogg's (Rice Krispies), and Ovaltine wanted out. (How many of you still have a Welch's jelly glass lying around?) In addition, the ratings were sagging: kids were becoming more sophisticated and there was a broader array of programs for them to watch.

Howdy Doody, nonetheless, will always be remembered as a true pioneer, and Bob

Smith as an innovator. A television time capsule would not be complete without a kinescope or two of the old show. Perhaps it *was* loud and just a bit too commercial, but, then again, Buffalo Bob never intended it to be educational, just a "bunch of fun" for kids. And that it was.

This publicity still features Howdy with airline ticket agent Karen Collins at Ft. Lauderdale, Florida, where Bob Smith lives.

TV or Not TV

AN IRREVERENT LOOK AT TELEVISION

Judy Ervin and Bart Andrews

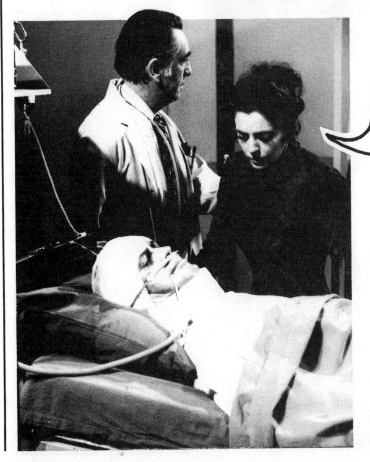

That Familiar Face

Many of your favorite performers have appeared in a number of TV series, portraying a variety of roles. In each case, name the personality who played all the roles indicated, and then the series in which he or she appeared in those roles.

1. An inexperienced owner of a photography studio; principal of Madison High School; next door neighbor to a brat; president of the Danfield National Bank.

2. A houseboat occupant; a Marine Corps private; the father of two kids and a chimpanzee; a reporter for *Newsview* magazine.

3. The manager of a tennis resort; producer of a TV variety show; Lumpy's old man; a television writer.

4. A California farmer; a high school student; a state senator; a conservative Washington, D.C. columnist.

5. A senile witch; a globe-trotting widow; a regular on *The Garry Moore Show*; a Jefferson City boarding house landlady.

6. The town blacksmith; an Indian in New York City; pilot of the *Enterprise*; a small-town detective.

7. The daughter of a pleasure boat owner; a British teenager; the "Sock It to Me" girl; a newlywed art student in San Francisco.

8. An assistant on the Overland Stage; a detective for World Securities Corporation; a Shiloh ranch hand; owner of the Golden Gate Casino.

9. An overbearing Jewish mother; maid for the president of a construction company; the den mother for a bevy of Las Vegas cuties; a police commissioner's housekeeper.

10. Host of *Laugh Line;* a TV comedy writer; Phoenix talk-show host; a member of the Carol Burnett company.

11. A millionaire; a master woodsman in 1754; Davy Crockett's sidekick; a private eye.

12. A mathematics professor; one of the Barkleys; a pickle factory entrepreneur; a private eye in New Orleans.

13. A practical-joking uncle; a partner in a law firm in California; the Munster family physician; the administrator of a small private hospital.

14. A New York detective; a police sergeant in Santa Luisa, California; the head of a fashion house; manager of a Santa Monica apartment building.

15. A TV soap opera producer; one of the Hansens; the father of a large brood; Don Adams' police sergeant boss.

And Now a Word From...

Match the major sponsor with the show or star.

1. Lipton Tea _____

2. Sylvania _____

3. Plymouth _____

4. Geritol _____

5. Clearasil _____

6. Kraft Foods _____

7. Texaco _____

8. Philip Morris _____

9. Kellogg's Sugar Pops _____

10. Ford _____

11. Camel cigarettes _____

12. Revlon _____

13. Listerine _____

14. Kodak _____

15. Boraxo _____

16. Campbell's Soups _____

17. Kent cigarettes _____

18. Chevrolet _____

19. Hazel Bishop _____

20. American Dairy Association _____

a. *The Ernie Ford Show*

b. *The Children's Hour*

c. *Disneyland*

d. *The Ed Sullivan Show*

e. Arthur Godfrey

f. *You'll Never Get Rich*

g. *American Bandstand*

h. Dinah Shore

i. *Richard Diamond, Private Detective*

j. *Beat the Clock*

k. *Wild Bill Hickok*

l. Milton Berle

m. *Lassie*

n. *Death Valley Days*

o. *I Love Lucy*

p. *The Gale Storm Show*

q. *Mr. and Mrs. North*

r. *Ted Mack's Original Amateur Hour*

s. *The Lawrence Welk Show*

t. *This Is Your Life*

Through the Looking Glass

A full-page newspaper ad featured the sad plight of a winsome, pigtailed little girl blubbering on the shoulder of her pouting, sad-eyed brother, with the warning: "There are some things a son or daughter *won't* tell you!"

Sounds pretty heavy. Was it concern over drugs, pregnancy, incest? Hardly. This advertisement appeared in more than 1,100 newspapers in November, 1950, when we weren't too concerned over drug abuse and premarital sex.

The copy continued: "Do you expect him to blurt out the truth—that he's really ashamed to be with the gang—because he doesn't see the television shows they see? . . . How can a little girl describe the bruise deep inside? Can you deny television to your family any longer?"

Yes, a commercial for TV, paid for by The American Television Dealers and Manufacturers Association. The group even printed the advice of a child guidance expert: "Youngsters today need television for their morale as much as they need fresh air and sunshine for their health."

Did the ad work? Did it sell sets? That's hard to determine, but available statistics do bear out the fact that there were only four million TVs in 1950, but ten million in 1951.

Public outrage halted the campaign after the first advertisement. A second, featuring a freckle-faced, tearful boy described as "the loneliest kid on the block," never made it to press.

People resented being "shamed" into buying a TV set. "I'll buy one when I'm good and ready," said one parent. Other mothers and fathers wanted to delay the purchase as long as possible, for moral reasons. Whatever the reason for *not* buying a set, the media manipulation was still strong.

Look at the ad on the opposite page. It appeared in the February 13, 1950, issue of *Life* magazine. Featuring William Boyd in his familiar western role, Hopalong Cassidy, at the height of his TV popularity, the advertisement sought to capture the attention of youngsters, most of whom were already diehard western fans.

On the next few pages we highlight a few TV sets being advertised before 1960, during the so-called Golden Age of Television.

1. This 1949 RCA Victor set carried the slogan: "You feel you're an 'eye witness' right at the scene of action." Price: $199.95

2. Admiral's 1951, 20-inch TV with "Dynamagic" radio and "triple play" phonograph.

3. A brand from the past (1951), this Crosley 16-inch set featured a "beautiful cabinet, available in Honduras mahogany veneer or blond wood." It was further promoted: "You'll enjoy sharp tuning with Crosley's Unituner."

4. The 1951 Raytheon with the 17-inch screen. "All you want in a fine set, today or tomorrow, is yours with Raytheon. Steady, razor-sharp pictures! Tune in John Cameron Swayze with the news."

5. "The Kent Ensemble," by RCA Victor in 1950, "a 16-inch television in a complete furniture setting for only $239.95."

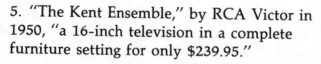

6. The ad read: "The front is all picture! It's brand new! It's sensational! With such amazing front row realism that you feel you can shake hands with the actors." The 21-inch Arvin (1955) cost $159.95.

7. 1955: Crosley's "Custom V 21 . . . with the difference you can see!"

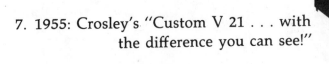

8. In 1950, this Motorola set was advertised as "not just *television,* but *Motorola* television. There's a Motorola to fit your budget . . . your home . . . your family."

20F1...huge 20-in.
rectangular tube,
FM/AM radio,
3-speed phono

9. "What finer gift could you give the whole family than a new RCA Victor TV. High and easy tuning hides controls in the top, on the sides, or behind closed doors on full-door models." This 1955 "Headliner 21" set: $199.95.

 NEEDS NO AERIAL—brings in beautifully clear sharp picture in all normal locations without an aerial of any kind, on a huge 97 square inch screen. Has the exclusive Philco luxury fea ire — the No-Glare Optical System that eliminates glare, makes television, at last, *easy on your eyes!* The new, exclusive Philco 3-speed automatic phonograph plays all kinds of records of all sizes, at all speeds automatically. You get more than 5 hours of continuous music. And the new Philco Super-Tone reproducer exerts just 1/5 ounce needle pressure on your records — gives you the finest tone ever achieved for recorded music. Plus the new Philco Super-powered AM-FM radio. All in a distinguished modern cabinet with full-length doors. Philco model 1479.

$499⁹⁵
Tax and
Warranty $11.75
*Price slightly
higher in far West*

10. Philco Model 1479 of 1949.

11. Philco Model 1400 of 1949.

NEEDS NO AERIAL in any normal location. New Philco super-sensitive television circuit and High Gain Tuner give you a clearer and sharper picture than ever on a huge 97 square inch screen. No high cost installation, and the price is nearly $200.00 less than last year's 90 square inch picture. Philco model 1400.

$259⁹⁵
Tax and
Warranty $3.80

Clearest "Big-Picture" detail ever

21" RCA Victor Suffolk. Super Set
with television's clearest, strongest,
big-screen pictures. Colonial-style
cabinet in walnut, mahogany finish.
Limed oak finish slightly higher.
Model 21T176, $425.

Zenith's Model X. Full 21" Cinébeam television with
Ciné-Lens, 20,000-volt Royal "R" chassis. Phonojack
for playing LP records. In Mahogany $379.95*. In
Blonde as shown, $389.95*. Top Tuning starts at $299.95*.

The royalty of radio and TELEVISION ®

Backed by 36 years of experience in radionics exclusively
ALSO MAKERS OF FINE HEARING AIDS
Zenith Radio Corporation, Chicago 39, Illinois

12. The RCA 21-inch Suffolk model of
1951, "with 'Picture Power!' You get the
matchless 'Golden Throat' tone system.
More people own RCA Victor than any
other make."

13. Winky Dink was featured in this 1954
Zenith ad: " 'You are there' reality. Now
you don't even bend over to click the dial.
And every 'click' brings you TV's sharpest
picture automatically."

How Well Do You Know the Bunkers?

AN *ALL IN THE FAMILY* CROSSWORD PUZZLE

ACROSS

2. Archie rarely acts his age: approximately——
5. One of Archie's words for blacks
9. Mike and Archie are usually "at——"
11. "Those Were the ——"
12. Archie's command to those sitting on 77 Across
13. ——Reiner
15. Family usually comes to Archie's ——
17. Archie roots for one
18. Street of former Bunker residence
20. Neighborhood bar
22. Betty Garrett plays her
23. Master of ceremonies (abbrev.)
25. Noise
26. An Archie-ism for a Jewish person
27. Anger
29. Archie's "shut up" to Edith
31. Performer who appeared as himself on series
33. Mike's nationality
36. Complain
37. She plays Gloria
39. Another smash CBS comedy series
40. Edith: Chief——and bottle washer
41. Archie's cousin who had the "audacity" to die at the Bunkers'
43. The Bunkers live here
44. Archie's initials
47. Night of the week show originally aired

49. Gloria's initials
51. Mike and Gloria ——
53. First name of 68 Across
56. Trick-or-treat month (abbrev.)
57. Show debuted on January twelfth, nineteen hundred seventy-——
58. Production company responsible for show
60. Form of address Lionel uses for Archie (abbrev.)
61. Next door neighbors
63. Horsepower (abbrev.)
64. Archie called this boxing champ a "black beauty"
66. Mark
68. Star of series *All in the Family* replaced
70. According to Archie, Mike would do this constantly
71. Likely form of address for Gloria
73. An Archie tag for a homosexual
74. Archie's favorite beverage
76. "Girls were girls and men were——"
77. Archie's "nest"
79. Sick
80. Mike would enjoy calling Archie this
81. Sixty minutes
83. One of the writers
85. Jean Stapleton's married name
87. Archie's favorite newspaper, *The Daily News,* has at least one in its classified section
88. Priest played by actor Barnard Hughes

89. Archie complains about the—— shortage
91. Same as 71 Across
92. Cost of bus or subway ride
93. Archie's hypocrisy
97. White Anglo-Saxon Protestant (abbrev.)
100. Another *Family* scribe
103. What Gloria calls Archie
104. Color of Archie's socks
106. The first name of this U.S. President caused Edith to assume he was Jewish
108. Archie's incessant plea to Mike: "——job!" (2 words)
110. Edith drinks Coca-——
112. Archie blames this race for 89 Across
113. He plays Archie
115. Mike calls Edith this
116. Where Mike spends his time
117. Archie Bunker: "TV's lovable——"
118. What Archie once had to buy from undertaker Whitehead

DOWN

1. Commie
3. Edith and Archie celebrated twenty-—— years of marriage in Atlantic City
4. Slang for "you people"
5. Some would call Edith this
6. Type of fans the program boasts

7. British series *'Til Death Us—Part*
8. Edith's initials
10. Archie's label for a person who doesn't agree with him
11. According to Archie, Edith is a ——
14. To get Mike's attention, Archie might shout this (2 words)
16. Nationality of 22 Across
19. State in which the Bunkers reside
21. Husband of 22 Across: Frank——
24. Archie often has one after dinner
28. Lyricist of closing song (initials)
30. Edith buys Archie's prunes at this market
32. Mike's hometown
33. Archie and Edith aren't likely to see any movie with a rating greater than this
34. Creator of *All in the Family*
35. Wouldn't be one of Archie's favorite comedians
37. How Archie might say yes to a Puerto Rican
38. One of Archie's days off
39. What Gloria calls Edith
40. The uncle who attended Mike and Gloria's wedding
42. Network
45. British network
46. He plays Lionel Jefferson on *Family*
48. Partner of 34 Down
50. One of Archie's co-workers

52. Archie occasionally "moonlights" as one
54. When it comes to religion, Mike considers himself one
55. Italian city where 21 Down comes from
59. Archie's Flushing IRT train rides on one
62. According to Archie, ribs, fried chicken, and watermelon belong in this food category
65. Lionel's uncle
67. ——*Death Us Do Part*
69. Not likely—an "Archie Bunker Admiration Society" (abbrev.)
71. Edith's liberal cousin from Westchester
72. How Archie would like all blacks to address him
75. Edith—"A real—— ——"
76. Archie's favorite baseball team
78. After an argument with Archie, you might be——
82. Street on which the Bunkers live
83. The world's shortest book, *The Wit and——of Archie Bunker*
84. Nixon's "—— and order" platform of 1972 caused Archie to vote for him
86. What Mike and Archie could use during verbal battles
90. Last syllable of Poland's capital
94. Probably will not

take the place of Archie's hat

95. Lyricist of opening theme song

96. When Gloria was

sick, they called one (abbrev.)

98. "Thou———not bear false witness against thy neighbor"

99. Archie Bunker-ism for Jewish people

101. Some might call Archie this

102. "Pull the plug on it"

105. Game Gloria played as a child

107. The size of Archie's mouth

109. ———in the Family

111. What a 54 Down

does not believe in

113. State from which 34 Down hails

114. Gloria might also have played this game as a kid: Hi

The Slings and Arrows
of Outrageous Cancellation

What is the effect of a TV cancellation on stars? For some, it's just another valley, an inevitability on the road to eventual success—something better is bound to come along. For others, starring in a dismal flop can spell the end of a career.

Four funny people, Tim Conway, Phyllis Diller, Don Rickles, and Jerry Van Dyke, share the dubious distinction of having appeared in more flop TV shows than just about anybody else. Ripley might not even believe it. Rickles has been more fortunate than most —he got another shot at the medium with *C.P.O. Sharkey* on NBC. Conway, on the other hand, has been content playing third banana to Carol Burnett until the star decided to retire from the weekly grind of television.

Here is a recent conversation with the flopping foursome.

ANDREWS: Miss Diller, in 1966 you did a sitcom for ABC called *The Pruitts of Southampton*. Why wasn't the show successful like, say *That Girl* or *Family Affair*, both of which also began that season?

DILLER: Everyone involved couldn't have cared less. Right from the beginning there was no strength, no muscle. Nobody gave it any attention. I remember one day our executive producer, David Levy, walked on the set and up to me and said, "Wear earrings." Here we had a show that was going down the drain and that's all he said. That was his total contribution to *Pruitts.* As far as I was concerned, it was the last straw. There was never any talk about changing writers or finding a new cast. Poor Grady Sutton [who played ancient butler Sturgis] was on his last leg and Reggie Gardiner was so sick he couldn't take the hot lights. And Gypsy Rose Lee, my dear friend who played my next door neighbor, couldn't stay within the confines of a script.

ANDREWS: Didn't they revamp the show in midseason, and give it a new title?

DILLER: By then it was too late. The show already had a bad name. Changing the title doesn't mean a damn thing. Even if you gift-wrap your garbage, it's still nothing but garbage.

ANDREWS: Would you say then that disinterest on the part of the production people is a prime reason for the failure of most series?

DILLER: Let me give you another example. When I did my variety show *(The Beautiful Phyllis Diller Show)* for NBC, the producers, who shall remain nameless, were too preoccupied with other projects. They came up with the concept but never showed up at the studio. Our executive producer was too busy trying to salvage Jerry Lewis's show at the time. I *never* saw him! To this day, I don't know what the man looks like! The show didn't mean a thing to anyone.

ANDREWS: How about you, Tim? You've starred in three series that failed before landing the assignment on Carol Burnett's show.

CONWAY: My first two series were situation comedies *(Rango* and *The Tim Conway Show)* and both were midseason replacements. And I don't know what happened, it happened so fast. None of my shows has lasted over thirteen weeks. (Conway's California license plates reads "13 WKS.") As for my variety show, I think

54

it was *too* clever. For instance, we did our Christmas show in September. Had Sally Struthers, long before *Family* went on the air, doing solo production numbers. Things like that. I knew we were doomed because every week we'd get a bunch of neatly-typed letters from Senators and Congressmen saying how clever we were. To stay on the air, you have to get letters written in Crayola and mailed with Green Stamps.

ANDREWS: Mr. Rickles, you appeared in a sitcom for CBS in which you played an advertising executive with a wife and daughter. It lasted only half a season. Why?

RICKLES: CBS wanted me to be a nice guy like Dick Van Dyke and Bob Newhart. I can't be a Van Dyke or a Newhart. There's no controversy, which my humor thrives on. The format was wrong for me. I think *Sharkey* is more in keeping with my style.

ANDREWS: Jerry Van Dyke, you did a series about a talking car *(My Mother, the Car)*. That was a pretty far-out concept, even a

dozen years ago. Did you think it was going to succeed before you went into it?

VAN DYKE: I had no faith in that show whatsoever. I took it because no one was offering me anything else.

ANDREWS: Why did you do *Accidental Family* a few years later? Wasn't that just as outrageous a premise?

VAN DYKE: I took that because of Sheldon Leonard (executive producer). Did I have confidence in it? Not really. The pilot script wasn't that sharp. But I thought that with Sheldon guiding the show it could be something. But he was too busy at the time with other things, and didn't get around enough. Plus the idea for the show was too complicated. If you didn't see the pilot episode which explained everything, forget it—you'd be lost.

ANDREWS: Besides wrong concepts and disinterested producers, what other reasons contributed to your various series disasters? What about time periods? Are they as important as we keep hearing?

DILLER: God, are they important! On *Pruitts,* I was sandwiched between *Love on a Rooftop* and *The Rounders.* None of us had a chance and we were all cancelled together, en masse.

ANDREWS: But your variety show had *Bonanza* as its lead-in, and that show was in the Top Ten.

DILLER: Yeah, but who watches TV so late (10 P.M.) on a Sunday when you have to get up for work or school the following day?

CONWAY: In the rating books, next to *my* shows, there was an asterisk saying "See below." And below, it said, "We can't find anybody watching this."

VAN DYKE: You talk about ratings and time

periods. For *Accidental Family,* we had the lousiest time slot going, bucking the *CBS Friday Night Movie.* Our first segment was up against *The Great Escape,* our second competed with Jimmy Stewart and John Wayne in *The Man Who Shot Liberty Valance,* and our third was pre-empted by President Johnson who gave a speech about Vietnam. After the first three weeks, I knew we were right in the toilet.

ANDREWS: It seems that all of you have the good fortune of scoring well as guest stars on other people's shows, rather than your own. Why do you think that is?

CONWAY: When you have your own series, no matter how successful you were in previous shows, people see you in a whole new light. "Hey," they say. "There he is up there with a fancy tuxedo. Now let's see what the big shot can do." It's like what happened with Don Knotts. Four or five Emmy awards for Andy Griffith's show and seventeen weeks on his own and nobody remembers a thing.

VAN DYKE: I've had my own shows and I've co-starred on other shows. Believe me, being in a flop—no matter whose it is—is bad, *bad* news. I was on *The Judy Garland Show* fifteen years ago and got fired. I was on Andy Griffith's *Headmaster* and got bounced by Thanksgiving. Talk about a turkey.

ANDREWS: Being cancelled, or fired. What's that like?

RICKLES: It's not the actual cancellation that bugs you, it's the waiting. They call you and say you got a 32 in Des Moines and you ask them what that means and they say it means you don't have a thing to worry about. Then someone else calls up and says you got a 13 in San Diego and you ask what that means and they say you better start worrying. It's very strange.

ANDREWS: Is that what happened with your CBS sitcom?

RICKLES: Yes. In the meantime, Sheldon Leonard, our executive producer, was

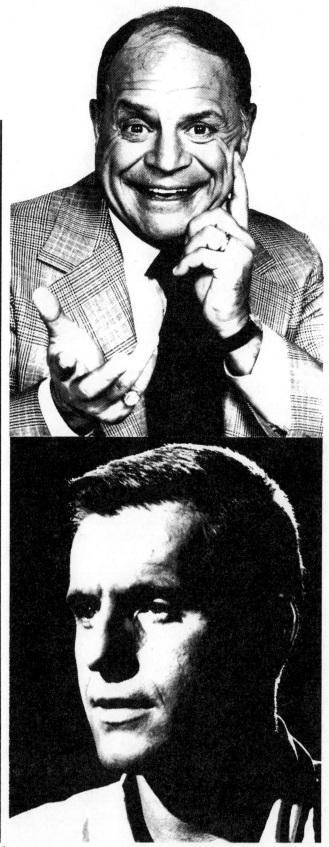

making plans for a trip to Europe and he said it'd be either a celebration or a wake. And there I was at home, sitting on the potty sweating while he was in Venice making a left turn on some canal saying, "I wonder if they've flushed The Kid down the toilet yet?"

VAN DYKE: The third time the bottom fell out of my TV career, during *Headmaster*, really hurt me. All of a sudden, I was totally out of work. No warning, no nothing. It was devastating. I was just about ready to sell the house and go back to Danville, Illinois, my hometown. No kidding. That really got to me, that last one. Because I knew what it meant to my career.

ANDREWS: Miss Diller, it's happened to you twice. What was the effect?

DILLER: It isn't that important. I have a nightclub act, and I do concerts and now I'm even doing symphonies.

ANDREWS: Are you saying that you don't care about television, that it isn't important to you?

DILLER: No. TV is a challenge. I'd like to succeed just once. I've succeeded in every other area of show business except starring on my own TV show. I'd love to do another series and make it stick.

CONWAY: Me? I love this business so much, it's all part of it. I hope I get another chance, and I think I will. But for the time being, I'm very satisfied that I've found a niche.

VAN DYKE: I *hope* I get another chance too. But I honestly doubt it. Let's face it, my television career leaves a lot to be desired. I was pretty hot when I started, but then to have cooled down the way I did.

RICKLES: I don't *need* TV, but I want it. I know I'm a star. I know I make big dough. I don't need the money. I'll take it, but I don't need it. I know I'm a success. I need more of it. I feed off it. I want a hot movie and I want the biggest TV show going.

ANDREWS: If you get another stab at television, is there anything you'll do differently?

VAN DYKE: I'd insist on a 3-camera show filmed before a live audience. I didn't have that before. I need the flow and the laughs. I'm not a one-camera artist. If there's an audience, I'll get the laughs. I'd also want to meet the writers beforehand, and know their work. But I don't think the idea itself for a show is that important; the combination of writing and performing is. A really good show will make it and I don't think any of my previous shows were any good.

DILLER: The next time? It won't go wrong the next time. I'd want to know what I'm getting into beforehand. Know the people, know everything.

CONWAY: All I know is one thing: If I get another show, I won't order any fancy script-binders. It takes thirteen weeks just to get them made up!

Big Game Hunt

Match the host with his game show.

1. Bud Collyer _____	a. *You Don't Say*
2. Allen Ludden _____	b. *I'll Bet*
3. Gene Rayburn _____	c. *Truth or Consequences*
4. Warren Hull _____	d. *College Bowl*
5. Peter Donald _____	e. *Beat the Clock*
6. Jack Bailey _____	f. *Concentration*
7. Hal March _____	g. *Two for the Money*
8. Johnny Carson _____	h. *The Quiz Kids*
9. George deWitt _____	i. *Earn Your Vacation*
10. Clifton Fadiman _____	j. *Alumni Fun*
11. Art Fleming _____	k. *Strike It Rich*
12. Bill Cullen _____	l. *The $64,000 Question*
13. Dick Clark _____	m. *Jeopardy*
14. George Fenneman _____	n. *The $10,000 Pyramid*
15. Jack Narz _____	o. *Eye Guess*
16. Tom Kennedy _____	p. *Masquerade Party*
17. Herb Shriner _____	q. *Your Surprise Package*
18. Merv Griffin _____	r. *Play Your Hunch*
19. Joe Kelly _____	s. *Match Game*
20. Hugh Downs _____	t. *Name That Tune*

THE DIVINE MISS EMMY

The first Television Academy Emmys were awarded in Hollywood, California, at the Athletic Club on January 25, 1949, covering the 1948 season. Only six Emmys were presented—one to a performer, two to programs—one "live" and one film— one to a local Los Angeles station, and a special award to Louis McManus, the man who designed the Emmy statuette. Over the years, the Emmy has become universally recognized and accepted as television's most distinguished and respected honor.

The Emmy got its name from Immy, the term used to describe the image orthicon camera tube, the type used on a TV camera. Years ago there was a rumor circulating which hinted that the Emmy was named for Faye Emerson, one of television's earliest personalities, but this is only conjecture.

Here is a quiz which tests your ability to recall the winners of various Emmys through the years. Identify the personality or program for the clues provided.

1948: The "Most Popular Television Program" was a game show with Mike Stokey as host.

1949: The "Best Children's Show" was created by Bob Clampett.

1950: The "Most Outstanding Personality" played host to a duck named Merdle.

1951: "Best Actor" co-starred with Howard Morris and the Billy Williams Quartet.

1952: The "Best Mystery, Action, or Adventure Program" had Ben Alexander as a regular.

1953: The "Best Public Affairs Program" featured a score by Richard Rodgers.

1954: "Best Variety Series" was produced by Walt Disney.

1955: The "Best Comedian" was featured on a show about military life.

1956: "Best Male Personality" wore sweaters and smoked Chesterfields.

1957: "Best Single Program of the Year" was a *Playhouse 90* drama starring Mickey Rooney.

THE DIVINE MISS EMMY

1958: The "Best Western Series" featured Jack Kelly as one of two gun-toting brothers.

1959: "Outstanding Achievement in the Field of Children's Programming" was the animated misadventures of a Hanna-Barbera-created canine.

1960: The "Program of the Year" was a Shakespearean presentation on *The Hallmark Hall of Fame.*

1961: "Outstanding Program Achievement in the Field of Drama" featured a cast of actors headed by E.G. Marshall.

1962: "Outstanding Continued Performance by an Actress in a Series" was won by an actress who brought a popular comic character to life.

1963: "Outstanding Program Achievement in the Field of Variety" was won by a program featuring Harvey Korman.

1964: "Outstanding Program Achievement in Entertainment" was won by a sitcom created by Carl Reiner.

1965: The "Outstanding Dramatic Series" was a Quinn Martin production about a fugitive.

1966: The "Outstanding Comedy Series" featured a quartet of young performers, one of whom was the star of *Circus Boy.*

1967: The "Outstanding Dramatic Series" was a Desilu production starring Steven Hill.

1968: "Outstanding Variety or Musical Series" featured a short clip of Richard Nixon saying "Sock it to *me?*"

1969: "Outstanding New Series" was set at Walt Whitman High School.

1970: "Outstanding Musical-Variety Series" featured a black star famous for his female impersonations.

1971: "Outstanding New Series" was a *Masterpiece Theatre* presentation.

1972: The "Outstanding Performance by an Actor in a Supporting Role in a Drama" was given by a young actor who played the son of a homosexual.

1973: "Best Lead Actor in a Limited Series" was the star of a Joseph Wambaugh novel.

1974: "Outstanding Lead in a Drama Series" was a former member of the *Our Gang* troupe.

1975: "Outstanding Comedy-Variety or Music Series" was a New York-based, live satirical revue.

Who Am I?

Animals are people, too. They have identities, especially in television. Can you recognize these "characters" from their own descriptions?

1. I was C.O.N.T.R.O.L.'s canine agent.

2. Sandy and Bud were my best friends.

3. Velvet Brown trained me for the Grand National Steeplechase.

4. I was the Munsters' fire-breathing dragon.

5. Ranger Cory Stuart adopted me after Cully became too ill to care for me.

6. I was the elephant of the Burke and Walsh Circus.

7. The Goose Bar Ranch was my home.

8. I was the Reynolds family pet chimp.

9. Mary Jane Croft lent her voice to me.

10. I lived at Gull Cottage in Maine.

11. I was Tammy Ward's favorite parrot.

12. Nick and Nora adopted me.

13. I was the mischievous chimpanzee at the Wameru Game Preserve and Research Center in Africa.

14. My mother was killed by a hunter in

the Florida Everglades, and I became Mark Wedloe's friend.

---

15. One of my masters was an adopted boy named Ernie Thompson.

---

16. We were Walter and Elinore Hathaway's three chimps.

---

17. I was Wilbur Post's palomino.

---

18. I was Joey Newton's equine friend.

---

19. My master was a "father" with a Chinese houseboy named Peter.

---

20. I was the pet lion on *The Addams Family*.

Friendly Persuasions

Can you identify the friends, relatives, employers, or associates of the following television characters?

1. Corliss Archer's boyfriend _____

2. Joan Stevens' sister _____

3. Rootie Kazootie's human friend_____

4. Sky King's nephew _____

5. Lucy Ricardo's mother_____

6. Mr. Peepers' girlfriend_____

7. Bob Beanblossom's boss _____

8. Connie Brooks' landlady_____

9. George Burns' mailman _____

10. Irma Peterson's roommate _____

11. Rosalee Goldberg's father _____

12. Beulah's best friend _____

13. Chester A. Riley's daughter _____

14. Samantha Stephens' family physician ___

15. Margie Albright's boyfriend _____

16. George Jetson's robot maid_____

17. Ben Cartwright's adopted son _____

18. Gidget Lawrence's married sister _____

19. Bob Collins' sister_____

20. Cosmo Topper's boss _____

Can You Picture This?

1. Don Knotts received five Emmys for his brilliant portrayal of Barney Fife on *The Andy Griffith Show.* Here he talks with his occasional girlfriend, Juanita. Where did she work? _____

2. Mary Stuart, star of *Search for Tomorrow,* has probably racked up more first-run television hours than any other actress in the United States. Since September 3, 1951, Ms. Stuart has been bringing joy (and sorrow) to Americans, young and old, as Joanne Gardner Barron Tate Vincent. Name the motel Joanne once owned. _____

3. Tab Hunter was destined for TV stardom, or so NBC thought. On September 20, 1960, *The Tab Hunter Show* debuted, but ran only one season. What cartoon did Malibu playboy Paul Morgan draw for a newspaper syndicate? _____

4. Buddy Blatner and this man hosted *Game of the Week* on CBS. Who is this sports announcer? _____

5. From vaudeville, movies, and radio, George Burns and Gracie Allen made their television debut on October 12, 1950. Among other features, Burns would often explain to the audience what was going on while the show was in progress. Bea Benadaret played neighbor Blanche Morton, but who played her husband Harry? _____

6. Ted Key's popular *Saturday Evening Post* cartoon, *Hazel,* came to the TV screen in 1961 with Shirley Booth as the lovable, but meddlesome maid. Under her care was young Harold Baxter, George and Dorothy's only son. Name the child actor who portrayed Harold._____

1.

2.

3.

4.

6.

5.

Can You Picture This?

7. Patrick McVey played Steve Wilson, a crime reporter, on *Big Town*. Jane Nigh portrayed his society reporter associate. Can you recall her name? _____

8. Mr. Lucky was the owner and operator of the *Fortuna,* a posh supper club and gambling yacht. With music by Henry Mancini, the show premiered on CBS in 1959. What was Lucky's real name, and who played him? _____

9. Premiering on September 24, 1964, *The Munsters* brought back to TV the team of Fred Gwynne and Al Lewis, who had been together on *Car 54, Where Are You?,* as Herman Munster and his funereal father-in-law. Yvonne DeCarlo played Lily

Munster, Herman's spouse. Where did this
unusual family live? _____

10. *The Detectives* debuted in 1959 and ran
three years before going into syndication.
Its illustrious cast was head by Robert
Taylor (seated). His co-stars all went on to
star in television series. Name them, and
their programs. _____

11. Sally Field played Sister Bertrille, a nun
who accidentally discovered that the
combination of her habit's design and the
Puerto Rican tradewinds gave her special
aerial abilities. What was Sister Bertrille's
name before she was ordained? _____

12. A radio staple since 1939, *Mr. District
Attorney* came to TV in 1951 with Jay Jostyn
playing the role he essayed on radio. After
Jostyn left, who inherited the role as
"Champion of the People"? _____

11.

12.

10.

13. Jim Nabors played a simple-minded marine on *Gomer Pyle, U.S.M.C.*, a 1964 spin-off of *The Andy Griffith Show.* Where was Gomer stationed, and who was his demanding drill sergeant? _____

14. *The Monroes* were five parentless children trying to survive in the West. How did Mr. and Mrs. Albert Monroe die?_____

15. Eve Arden starred as Connie Brooks, an English teacher at Madison High, on *Our Miss Brooks.* Who played Philip Boynton, the object of her affections? _____

16. Who is this petticoated woman and for what was she most famous? _____

17. Neville Brand, Peter Brown, and William Smith starred in *Laredo,* a 1965 western. What law enforcement group were they members of? _____

18. Mike Stokey's *Pantomime Quiz* premiered October 4, 1949, and was on and off the network for ten years, often during the summer. Home viewers were rewarded for suggesting charades. How much time was allowed to solve one of these "stumpers"?

_____

19. *My Living Doll* starred Bob Cummings as a psychiatrist who was assigned the task of properly programming the U.S. Space Project AF 709, a beautiful female robot played by Julie Newmar. What was the robot's nickname? _____

20. *Daktari* was a 1966 entry with Marshall Thompson as an African game preserve director. What does the Swahili word "daktari" mean? _____

21.

23.

22.

21. In a Bronx apartment, a close knit
Jewish family struggled to make ends meet.
From radio to television, this compassionate
series warmed many hearts. Name the
series, the actor pictured, and his character.
(Hint: He played the same role in a recent,
but unsuccessful Broadway musical.) _____

22. Barbara Stanwyck made the big switch
to television in 1965 with *The Big Valley*.
She played Victoria Barkley, a widow
trying to manage a 30,000-acre ranch near
Stockton, California. Name her five
children, one of whom was her husband's
illegitimate son by an Indian maiden. _____

23. Gale Gordon and Bob Sweeney worked
together in *Our Miss Brooks* so well that they
were given their own series in 1956 called
The Brothers. What were Harvey and
Gilmore's last name? _____

24. On his way to work at the *Los Angeles
Sun*, Tim O'Hara discovered a crashed UFO
and its passenger. *My Favorite Martian* was a
1963 sitcom about the friendship between
the earthling and the Martian, who posed
as Tim's Uncle Martin. What was Uncle
Martin's profession on Mars? _____

25. Eloise McElhone and Robin Chandler
were panelists on *Leave It to the Girls*, and
Maggi McNellis was the moderator of this
early 1950s program. What was the show's
format? _____

24.

25.

THE GAME GAME

On July 1, 1941, commercial TV broadcasting began. Among the few shows airing that summer day were *Uncle Jim's Question Bee* and *Truth or Consequences,* both rehashed radio programs, both game shows. The genre is, obviously, one of the medium's earliest forms. This quiz tests your knowledge of this broadcasting staple.

Identify the game show from these clues.

1. Imposters try to fool celebrity panelists.

2. Contestants hope to win twenty silver dollars by correctly answering questions.

3. Players must provide the question to the answer given.

4. Celebrities are disguised by ingenious make-up techniques.

5. Contestants vie for a houseful of furniture.

6. Panelists are shown objects from the past, and must identify them.

7. Elaborate, timed stunts are performed by contestants.

8. Heartbreaking stories are told in an effort to win needed prizes.

9. Contestants hope to correctly guess the retail value of items.

10. Players try to answer correctly a "hard" or "easy" question.

11. Contestants choose two numbers on a large playing board, hoping to match hidden prizes, and solve a rebus.

12. Two contestants compete for a large piece of a puzzle.

13. Tic-tac-toe.

14. Two contestants and one athlete combine forces to win prizes and set new records.

15. A test of the five senses.

16. Contestants pick three "ideal" members of the opposite sex, then narrow it down to one perfect date.

17. Players try to identify the author of a famous quotation.

19. Contestants trade their homemade articles for cash or valuable prizes.

18. Two teams compete in a game of charades.

20. Celebrity couples reveal secrets about themselves.

The "Are You a TV Addict?" Test

What are your attitudes toward the tube? How do you react during a television crisis? Are you emotionally stable enough to own a color set? Answer honestly the following multiple-choice questions and determine, once and for all, whether you are hooked on television.

1. Your three favorite TV shows are on at the same time. Would you:
   a. Choose one, and promise yourself you'll see the others in rerun? _____
   b. Watch none, considering it a form of corporal punishment?_____
   c. Rush out and buy two more TV sets so you can watch all of them?_____
   d. Flip back and forth between all three, trying to catch the best parts? _____
2. Your idea of the perfect meal is:
   a. A TV dinner. _____
   b. Chinese food, because you can eat every half-hour. _____
   c. Veal cordon bleu. _____
   d. Take-out pizza. _____
3. You are out on a date, and it is approaching 11 P.M., the time you usually watch television. Do you:
   a. Fall asleep, hoping your date will take the hint? _____
   b. Bring along a portable television set and a big supply of batteries? _____
   c. Consider finding a new friend, one who shares your interest in television? __
   d. Enjoy yourself and forget about TV?

   _____
4. Your favorite magazine is:
   a. *TV Guide.* _____
   b. *Time.* _____
   c. *The National Review.* _____
   d. *Holiday.* _____
5. Your favorite television program has been cancelled. Do you:
   a. Wear a dark suit for the next thirteen weeks? _____

   b. Watch something else?_____
   c. Turn in your membership card to the human race?_____
   d. Write nasty letters to the network? __
6. If you were waiting for a friend to finish shopping in a department store, you would bide your time in the:
   a. TV department. _____
   b. Book section. _____
   c. Ladies ready-wear._____
   d. Furniture department. _____
7. Your idea of the perfect vacation spot is:
   a. Burbank, California, home of NBC-TV. _____
   b. The South of France. _____
   c. Borneo._____
   d. New York City where there are seven TV stations. _____
8. You've just had twins, a boy and a girl. Would you name them:
   a. John and Mary? _____
   b. Ozzie and Harriet? _____
   c. Tee and Vee? _____
   d. Buffy and Jody?_____
9. You hate to admit to your friends that you watch television, but when pressured, you tell them you watch:
   a. *Meet the Press.* _____
   b. Public broadcasting. _____
   c. *I Love Lucy,* claiming you're a purist and that *Lucy* is a classic in the genre. __
   d. Test patterns. _____
10. You are watching television and your loved one is in a romantic mood. Do you:
    a. Tell him/her to wait until the next commercial? _____

b. Shut off the TV? _____

c. Wait until the station signs off for the day? _____

d. Have a go at it, but continue watching TV? _____

HOW TO SCORE YOURSELF

Give yourself the points indicated below.
1. a. no points, b. 5 points, c. 10 points, d. 8 points
2. a. 10 points, b. 8 points, c. no points, d. 5 points
3. a. 8 points, b. 10 points, c. 5 points, d. no points
4. a. 10 points, b. 8 points, c. no points, d. 5 points
5. a. 8 points, b. no points, c. 10 points, d. 5 points
6. a. 10 points, b. 5 points, c. 10 points, d. 8 points
7. a. 10 points, b. 5 points, c. no points, d. 8 points
8. a. no points, b. 8 points, c. 10 points, d. 5 points
9. a. no points, b. 5 points, c. 10 points, d. 8 points
10. a. 8 points, b. no points, c. 10 points, d. 5 points

IF YOUR TOTAL SCORE IS

0–39:   You know what a television is, all right, but you have difficulty finding the on/off knob.

40–69:   You enjoy TV, but do so in moderation.

70–89:   You are a definite television fan. Better renew your library card and read a book now and then.

90–100:   You are a TV addict of the first order. The sooner you face up to this, the better off you will be, weirdo.

REMEMBER...?

Television is old enough to have its own stars of yesterday, performers familiar for a season or two, or ten, who no longer appear regularly. Ready for a fast round of Where Are They Now?

AUDREY MEADOWS. During her six-year stint as Alice Kramden, Jackie Gleason's long-suffering TV spouse on *The Honeymooners,* she received thousands of aprons, potholders, and, yes, curtains from concerned fans. The truth is, Audrey Meadows is about as far removed from that character as any actor could be. "I loved Alice with her heart of gold and tongue of acid," she says, "but face it, she was a one-line character." Today Meadows lives with her husband, Continental Airlines President Bob Six, in a Park Avenue apartment and in the couple's luxurious Beverly Hills home. She travels extensively with Six, makes occasional TV appearances like the recent *Honeymooners* reunion specials, and truly enjoys her role as a housewife much more than that of a TV star.

JAY NORTH. Personally chosen at the age of seven by cartoonist Hank Ketcham for the title role in the CBS comedy, *Dennis the Menace,* Jay became an instant celebrity as the mischievous Master Mitchell. He earned about $600, plus residuals, for every one of the 146 episodes of the series, and later starred in two motion pictures as a juvenile. In 1967, he returned to TV, as a 15-year-old, in NBC's *Maya,* a short-lived adventure show shot in India. Since then, Jay experienced trouble securing acting assignments because of his Dennis image. So, in January of 1977, he enlisted in the Navy and began his four-year hitch with basic training in Orlando, Florida. "I'm not going to sit around Hollywood for the rest of my life waiting for a part," said Jay, who

hopes to go into law enforcement work after he completes his present tour of duty.

FAYE EMERSON. One of early TV's most familiar faces, she made frequent headlines because of the low-cut gowns she liked to wear, and because of her frequent marriages (Elliott Roosevelt and Skitch Henderson, among them). A television staple since 1948, Miss Emerson appeared as a panelist on *Leave It to the Girls* and *I've Got a Secret,* substituted frequently for Arlene Francis, Garry Moore, and Edward R. Murrow, on their respective shows, and wrote a popular TV column for United Press syndicate. In 1963, she took a year's leave of absence from her TV chores to travel in Europe. To the surprise of everyone, she has never returned. After a few years in Switzerland, she now lives in a four-bedroom home in Majorca. She has not remarried, and has no interest in returning to show business or the States.

HORACE HEIDT. A bandleader since the 1920s, he came to television in 1950 after a long and very successful career in radio. Heidt had a knack for discovering talented newcomers, and he brought to the small screen his *Youth Opportunity Program* in 1950 on CBS. In 1953, Horace decided to quit the band business, and devote all of his time to his real estate investments in the San Fernando Valley. Today, he is the resident landlord of a 170-unit apartment complex in Van Nuys, California, and has had the distinction of serving as the town's Mayor for many years.

IRISH MC CALLA. Filmed in Mexico, this woman's answer to Tarzan adventures, *Sheena, Queen of the Jungle,* had a short, but memorable run of twenty-six episodes during the mid-1950s. Tall and willowy, Ms. McCalla performed her jungle escapades clad only in a leopard loincloth. Her last foray into show business was in 1962 when she gave it up to devote all of her time to painting. Today, she lives in a small house on the beach at Malibu, teaches art at a local college, and is happy that her career as an artist has flourished.

AL HODGE. "The Guardian of the Safety of the World," better known as Captain Video, was one of television's first super-heroes. Decades ahead of *Star Wars,* this space fantasy aired five-days-a-week on the DuMont network, starring Hodge in the title role. After six seasons of interplanetary travel, the Captain was retired, and, for all intents and purposes, so ended Hodge's acting career. Hopelessly typecast, he found it almost impossible to find acting jobs, except some occasional commercial dubbing assignments in New York where he lives modestly. He no longer "rockets from planet to planet defending justice, truth, and freedom throughout the universe."

FACE IT

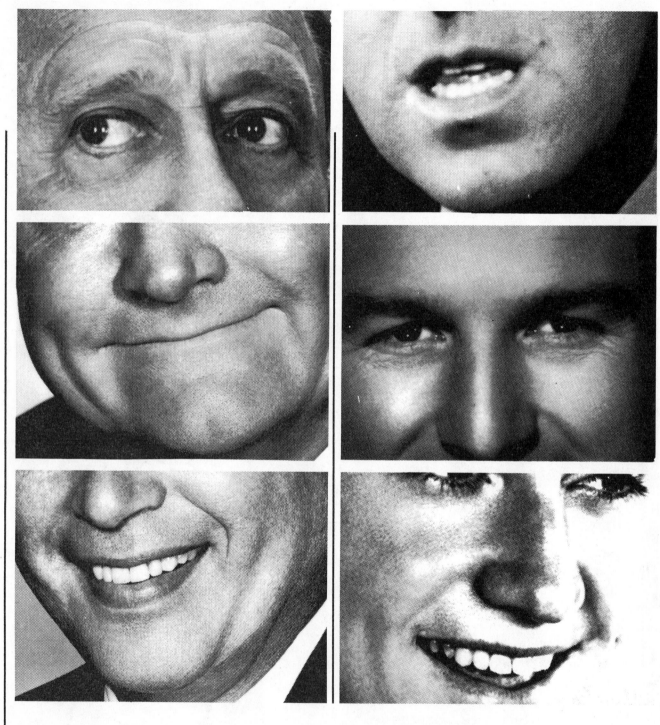

Can you identify the TV actors from just the portions of their faces?

1. _____ 2. _____

3. _____ 4. _____

5. _____ 6. _____

7. _____ 8. _____

9. _____ 10. _____

11. _____ 12. _____

13. _____ 14. _____

And Now for the $64,000 Question

Twelve-year-old Gloria Lockerman won $16,000 for spelling every word in the sentence, "The belligerent, astigmatic anthropologist annihilated innumerable chrysanthemumas"; Mrs. Myrtle Power, a 71-year-old housekeeper grandmother from Georgia, went home $32,000 richer because she was able to "name the six players in baseball, besides Ty Cobb, who had a lifetime total of 3,000 or more hits"; and Captain Richard McCutcheon, a Marine whose category was "Food and Cooking," who was asked to describe the menu served at Buckingham Palace on March 21, 1939 when King George VI and Queen Elizabeth entertained the President of France, won $64,000.

The setting was CBS Studio 52 in New York City and the show, of course, was *The $64,000 Question,* which premiered June 7, 1955, with Hal March as emcee. It was an instant success. By August, its ratings had doubled those of Ed Sullivan's variety show—an estimated 47,560,000 viewers were watching. The show was so popular that 15,000 letters arrived each week from fans who hoped to become contestants— only thirty of them were answered.

Besides Spelling, Baseball, and Food and Cooking, categories included The Bible, American History, Jazz, Mythology, Drama, Geography, Famous Pets, Literature, The Funnies, Opera, Pop Music, Artists, Headline Events, Gilbert and Sullivan, and Mark Twain.

Dr. Bergen Evans, then professor of English at Northwestern University, was the chairman of the board of editors which prepared all the questions. We have provided full quizzes for five categories: The Funnies, Great Books, Movies, American History, and Animals. Choose your category (if you're an all-around genius, try them all), and see if you might have been $64,000 richer back in the 1950s.

"THE FUNNIES"

Name the artist who currently draws these funnies.

$64 — *Joe Palooka* _____
$128 — *Mandrake the Magician* _____
$256 — *Out Our Way* _____
$512 — *Little Mary Mixup* _____

You have reached the First Plateau. . . . We have watched the Bumsteads raise a family in that realistic and subtle gem of the funnies, *Blondie.* Certain elements are always reliably the same, such as Dagwood's problems with his boss. For . . .

$1,000 — Name the irascible, kindly, and confused employer. _____

For a quarter of a century, we have chortled over the world created by Fontaine Fox. It features a swaying trolley car, believable but outrageous characters like Mickey McGuire, and a wonderful sense of humor. For . . .

$2,000 — Name Fontaine Fox's imaginary village._____

Clifford McBride created a lovable, bumbling bachelor and his Irish wolfhound. The huge and appealing dog is convinced that he is as cute and cuddly as a toy poodle and as heroic and efficient as Sir Galahad with an MIT degree. He is neither and his harassed owner has his troubles. For . . .

$4,000 — Who is the patient possessor of the pet, and what is the name of the charming monster? _____

Congratulations, you have reached the Second Plateau. . . . *Our Boarding House* exposes one of the great phonies of the American scene. He doesn't seem to fool his wife or the other long-suffering residents of the Boarding House, but he certainly keeps trying. For . . .

$8,000 — 1. Who is this appealing sham who hasn't found a buyer for his gold bricks since 1921? _____
2. What is his wife's name? ____

THE $64,000 QUESTION

Popeye the Sailor Man was a latecomer to the comic strip, *Thimble Theatre*. It started with the adventures of Ham Gravy and girl friend Olive Oyl. Popeye appeared in 1929. For . . .

$16,000 — 1. Who was Olive Oyl's brother? _____
2. Who is the hamburger-devouring little man, and what was his job when he was first seen on *Thimble Theatre?* _____
3. Who created *Thimble Theatre?*

_____

The Gumps were created for Captain Paterson, dynamic newspaper publisher, by a comic artist who had been doing strips like *Old Doc Yak* and *Buck Nix.* The members of the Gump family should be familiar to us all; they've been having adventures since the early twenties. For . . .

$32,000 — 1. What is the name of the Gumps' rich uncle? _____
2. What are the names of the two leading Gumps? _____
3. Who is their son and who is their maid? _____
4. Who created the characters?

_____

In 1892, a feature called *The Little Bear and Tigers* began to appear regularly in a western newspaper. Their cavortings interested readers and made many friends for the paper. They paved the way for later strips; perhaps even for Walt Disney. For . . .

$64,000 — 1. Who was their creator, who later drew another popular funny? _____
2. What newspaper first offered them to the public? _____
3. What comic strip did their creator draw later? _____

And Now for the $64,000 Question

"GREAT BOOKS"

From these capsule descriptions, name the book and its author.

$64 — A probe into the actions of a compulsive alcoholic over a forty-eight-hour period. _____

$128 — The antics and explosions of a dignified but unrepressed New Yorker and his family around the turn of the century._____

$256 — 1955's best-selling novel about a medical idealist who admitted to no barriers in his struggle to practice medicine. _____

$512 — This history of a foundling, written in 1749 is one of the great realistic novels in the English language. _____

You have reached the First Plateau. . . . Charles Dickens created some of the most striking characters in literature. In *A Tale of Two Cities,* a lady incites the mob to riot and sits calmly knitting during the worst scenes of the revolution. For . . .

$1,000 — Who is this wine-shop keeper created by Dickens?_____

In 1887, Edward Bellamy wrote a book about a man who is hypnotized into a state of animated suspension for a hundred and thirteen years. He awakes to find a marvelously advanced society of the year 2000 A.D. For . . .

$2,000 — Name this best-seller. _____

The Brothers Karamazov has the distinction of being Marilyn Monroe's favorite story. It is, besides, a penetrating psychological study by a brilliant author. For . . .

$4,000 — Is the author Dostoevsky, Tolstoy, or Franz Werfel? _____

Congratulations, you have reached the Second Plateau. . . . *Don Quixote* is familiar to us all as the tale of a gentle and eager knight errant who jousts with windmills and yearns to rescue damsels in distress. His illusions are constantly being buffeted by the common sense of his trusty follower. For . . .

$8,000 — 1. Who wrote *Don Quixote of La Mancha?* _____
2. What is the name of Quixote's follower? _____
3. Within twenty-five years, when was this two-part book published? _____

Upton Sinclair created a stir with the publication of a merciless probe into the meat-packing industry in 1906. He was one of the early group of "muckrakers" who forced reforms by informing the public. Thirty-seven years later he received a Pulitzer award for one volume in his *Lanny Budd* series. For . . .

$16,000 — 1. Name his book about the meat packers. _____
2. Name the book for which he received the Pulitzer Prize. _____

Pulitzer Prize winner, *The Way West,* deals with the men who pushed back the frontier of the United States. It examines them and the land they found with tremendous insight and graphic detail. For . . .

$32,000 — 1. Who was the author? _____

2. In what year did he receive the Pulitzer Prize? _____

3. What is the name of another book he wrote, published in 1947, that also deals with men who pushed back the frontier of the United States?_____

A distinguished member of a great American family looked back upon his life and education, and then wrote a book about them. It was published in the early 1900s and contains references to the great art and people known intimately by the author. His thesis was that he had been equipped with an eighteenth-century education to cope for a twentieth-century life. For . . .

$64,000 — 1. What is the book by this pessimistic, urbane scion?_____

2. What was the exact year of publication? _____

3. What was the profession of the author? _____

"MOVIES"

From these descriptions, recall the movies.

$64 — A story of late love in Venice, starring Katharine Hepburn. _____

$128 — Jane Wyman portrayed a deaf mute with an Oscar-winning performance._____

$256 — Robert Donat created an English schoolteacher for this one._____

$512 — Luise Rainer was a Chinese peasant in this movie version of a Pearl Buck novel._____

Congratulations, you have reached the First Plateau. . . . A cycle of documentary stories was started when this picture was filmed in New York. It described the round-trip of an espionage ring. William Eythe played an American double agent. For . . .

$1,000 — Name this picture. _____

Bob Hope, Bing Crosby, and Dorothy Lamour have traveled along many a road in pictures. The original *Road* picture was made in 1940. For . . .

$2,000 — Was it *Road to Morocco, Road to Singapore,* or *Road to Zanzibar*? _____

The Philadelphia Story was a brilliant stage success in 1939. Philip Barry's play was an equally bright part of the movie scene in 1940. For . . .

$4,000 — Name the three top stars of this movie. _____

Congratulations, you have reached the Second Plateau. . . . Shirley Temple entered the hearts of moviegoers in 1934. She was seen briefly in *Stand Up and Cheer* and then played a star role in a Damon Runyon story. For . . .

$8,000 — Name this picture and explain the title. _____

Daddy Long Legs was being shown in theatres in 1955. It was being shown back in 1918, too, with the current feminine favorite. For . . .

$16,000 — Who was the feminine star of the 1918 version of *Daddy Long Legs*? _____

On February 8, 1915, the motion picture industry attained a new stature as an art form. *The Birth of a Nation* gave the public excitement, a message, great sweeping battle scenes, and realism. For . . .

$32,000 — Who was the man who produced and directed this epic film? _____

Mack Sennett created the Keystone Cops and with them produced some of the funniest sequences in film history. For . . .

$64,000 — Name any *four* of the Keystone Cops of the 1914 crew. _____

"AMERICAN HISTORY"

$64 — What president never married? _____

$128 — What president arranged for the purchase of the Louisiana Territory? _____

$256 — Which state is the birthplace of more presidents than any other? ___

$512 — What president became a member of the Supreme Court after leaving the White House? _____

Congratulations, you have reached the First Plateau. . . . Columbus discovered America when he landed at an island in the West Indies. For . . .

$1,000 — What did he name the island on which he landed? _____

South Carolina was the first southern state to issue an "Ordinance of Secession." Six other states seceded from the Union by February, 1861. For . . .

$2,000 — Name *five* of those six states. _____

The United States purchased Alaska for the sum of $7,200,000. For . . .

$4,000 — 1. What year was the Treaty of Purchase signed? _____
2. Who was President? _____
3. From what nation did we purchase Alaska? _____

Congratulations, you have reached the Second Plateau. . . . In 1869, two railroads met at Promontory, Utah. The connection of their lines established the first transcontinental railroad. For . . .

$8,000 — Name both of the railroads. _____

The forty-sixth state joined the Union in 1907, the forty-seventh and forty-eighth in 1912. For . . .

$16,000 — Name these three states. _____

The first ten amendments to the Constitution of the United States are popularly known as the Bill of Rights. They guarantee certain basic freedoms and safeguards to the citizens of the United States. For . . .

$32,000 — Name the subject matter, or the most important provisions, of any *eight* of these amendments.

Ten men have served as Vice-President of the United States and then have become President. For . . .

$64,000 — Name them. _____

"ANIMALS"

If a sorority of lionesses (female lions) were having a dance, they would invites lions. Describe whom these female animals would invite.

$64 — Hens_____
$128 — Cows _____
$256 — Geese _____
$512 — Ducks_____

Congratulations, you have reached the First Plateau. . . . Tigers are more closely related to lions than they are to ostriches. For . . .
$1,000 — Is a bat most closely related to an owl, a butterfly, or a cow? __

Two of the following four animals are real, and two are imaginary. For . . .
$2,000 — Choose the two *real* animals among these four: the unicorn, the grampus, the wivern, and the potto. _____

Bees and wasps (including hornets) are social insects. They live in colonies and work together. For . . .
$4,000 — Name *two* other social insects. __

Congratulations, you have reached the Second Plateau. . . . Whales are warm-blooded mammals who breathe air into lungs, unlike fish whose environment they share. "Thar she blows" is an old whaling cry describing the surfacing of a whale to discharge used air before taking a fresh breath. For . . .
$8,000 — Does the average whale usually rise to breathe every five to ten minutes, every four to six hours, or every ten to twelve hours? __

The migratory flights of birds take them through storms and unknown dangers over vast distances. The champion migrant covers about 22,000 miles every year in order to spend the winter in a more southerly climate. For . . .
$16,000 — Name the bird who winters in the Antarctic and returns to the far North to nest. _____

The wolverine is a sharp-toothed, viciously clawed denizen of northern and arctic North America. For . . .
$32,000 — 1. What other name is given this animal?_____
2. How does he keep other animals from eating his kill? __
3. To what family of animals does he belong? _____

One of the animals most associated with the history of the American West is consistently called by the wrong name. He is saved from extinction only by strict government regulation. For . . .
$64,000 — 1. Give both this animal's true name and his commonly used name. _____
2. Within five million, how many of these animals are estimated to have lived in North America at their peak? __
3. Within ten percent, about how many do you think remain?_____

Little Known Facts About Big Name TV Stars

ED SULLIVAN

The first CBS press release, dated May 21, 1948, read: "Top-ranking performers in New York nightclubs, hotels and stars of movies, stage and radio are to be participating guests of Ed Sullivan, syndicated newspaper columnist, in a full-hour Sunday revue series titled *You're the Top,* and tentatively scheduled to begin on CBS June 20, 1948. . . ."

The title did not survive the first outpouring of publicity. The show premiered as *The Toast of the Town* on schedule, live from the Maxine Elliott Theatre in New York. It took thirty-five people to get the show on the air, *including* Ray Bloch's fourteen-member orchestra. The total budget: $1,500.

Among the opening night guests were Dean Martin and Jerry Lewis who split $200; pianist Eugene List who took home $75; six June Taylor dancers named "The Toastettes" who got twenty dollars apiece; and Richard Rodgers and Oscar Hammerstein, II who appeared gratis.

At the end of the first year of production, the show *cost* Sullivan $378 out of his own pocket. He admitted that he had been victimized by the small print in his CBS contract.

After only ten years on the air (the show lasted until 1971), Ed had employed more than 10,000 show business personalities, an incredible figure by any standards, allowing him the rightful status of impressario supreme.

GARRY MOORE

CBS and Thomas Garrison Morfit had a good thing going. Morfit, better known as Garry Moore, made a lot of money for CBS (during the early 1950s, he had sixteen simultaneous sponsors), and Garry made a lot of money off CBS.

In fact, according to the *Guinness Book of World Records,* Moore is the highest paid interviewer in the history of the medium. During Moore's banner year, 1963, when he was hosting *I've Got a Secret,* starring in his own nighttime variety show, and doing a daily radio show, all for CBS, he was pulling down $43,000 a week, or $2,236,000 for the year. Not bad for a guy who once co-authored a play with F. Scott Fitzgerald which was never produced.

Moore's long and profitable tenure with CBS came to an abrupt end in 1964 when the then president of the network, James Aubrey, better known in industry circles as "The Smiling Cobra," cancelled the star's variety show. Moore had admitted that the show was getting a little "old-hat," but had offered Aubry another idea, a fresh approach for a new program. Aubrey, who seemed to relish telling stars they were washed up (he once called Jack Benny and said simply, "You're through"), looked at Moore and said: "Not a chance." A few weeks later, Moore had no show at all.

Ironically, a year later, Aubrey was canned, too, and the following year (1966), Moore had his show back. Unfortunately, the magic wasn't there (neither was Carol Burnett), and it was cancelled in midseason.

ARTHUR GODFREY

On December 6, 1948, Arthur Godfrey began his second CBS series (the first was *Arthur Godfrey's Talent Scouts*), *Arthur Godfrey and Friends,* a Wednesday night hour that ran seven seasons. Among Godfrey's "friends" were Pat Boone, the McGuire Sisters, Marion Marlowe, Janette Davis, Haleloke, Carmel Quinn, the Mariners, and Julius LaRosa.

Singer LaRosa recalls a prophetic announcement made by Godfrey at a cast meeting early in 1953: "Remember," the redhead told his minions, "that many of you are here over the bodies of people I have personally slain. I have done it before and I can do it again!"

Several months later, on October 19, Godfrey introduced Julie to his TV audience (once estimated at 82 million) and said: "You're doing pretty good, aren't you? Getting big money in nightclubs, and so forth. This show must be a pain in the neck to you." LaRosa properly protested (even

though he was getting a paltry $191 a week, which was scale at that time), then sang the obligatory end song. When the applause died down, Godfrey smiled at his studio audience. "Thank you, Julie," he told the Italian crooner. "And that, folks, was Julie's swan song."

"Lack of humility" is the well known reason for the dismissal. But why did Godfrey choose this rather unconventional, rather cruel method? "I had the right to fire him on the air because I hired him on the air," Godfrey reasoned.

Arthur was also one of the first people to let Anita Bryant sing on television.

LUCILLE BALL

A funny thing happened to Lucille Ball on her way to becoming the First Lady of Television. She almost didn't make it.

When CBS asked Lucy to transfer her *My Favorite Husband* radio series to television in 1950, it was with the stipulation that she share co-star billing with Richard Denning, her airwaves spouse. Lucy had other ideas: namely Desi Arnaz, her husband.

But William S. Paley, CBS chieftain, didn't like her idea, and told her to stick to her movie career because nobody would ever believe that a typical, redheaded American girl could be married to a Latin, especially in a domestic comedy series.

Aside from the fact that she and Desi had been married, in *real life,* for ten years, Miss Ball considered Paley's concern ludicrous. So she had her radio writers, Bob Carroll, Jr. and Madelyn Pugh, concoct a

stage act for her and Desi to perform in key cities across the country, and, in June, 1950, the Arnazes assaulted New York, Chicago, San Francisco, and Milwaukee with their "vaudeville" act, and in a word, wowed 'em.

Armed with positive press reviews, Lucy approached Paley again. "The public believes we can be husband and wife," she told the CBS mogul.

"So do I," countered Paley. "Do your show."

EDWARD R. MURROW

About his successful CBS program, *Person to Person,* he once revealed, "To do the show I want to do [*See It Now*], I have to do the show that I don't want to do." Murrow considered his interview program "pure pap," but fully realized that pap was popular.

From its inception on October 2, 1953, (baseball great Roy Campanella was the first guest) *Person to Person* was a consistent ratings winner. Each half-hour show required the services of fifteen to twenty field technicians (directors, cameramen, sound experts, etc.), cost $25,000 to produce, and began with Edward Roscoe Murrow staring into the CBS camera, saying, "The name of the program is *Person to Person.*"

Some of those "persons" included Liberace, Eddie Fisher and Debbie Reynolds, the Duke and Duchess of

Windsor (she played jacks), Admiral Richard Byrd, Billy Graham, and Ed's last guest (June 26, 1959), Lee Remick.

Rin Tin Tin was once seriously proposed as a subject, but Murrow rejected the idea: "Lassie might ask for equal time, and some of our other guests might suffer by comparison."

MILTON BERLE

In 1948, the Texas Company decided to go into television and their Kudner advertising agency sold them on a vaudeville type show. The idea was to use a different emcee every four weeks, with Milton Berle as the starting host. *The Texaco Star Theatre* boasted seven other emcees during the first few months, including Ray Bolger, William Gaxton, Georgie Price, and Harry Richman.

It didn't take Texaco too long to realize that Berle was their best bet.

The show was a melange of brash, mostly loud entertainment. It was live every Tuesday night. It was unpredictable.

"Once we had on three trained elephants, and by the time their act was finished, the stage was covered with crap," Berle recalls. "Before we had a chance to clean it up, Jack Cole and the Kraft Sisters, our dancers, came on. At every turn, they stepped in it. We had a lot of acts that were hard to follow."

JACKIE GLEASON

One afternoon in 1951, Jackie Gleason suggested to his *Cavalcade of Stars* (DuMont Network) writers, Joe Bigelow and Harry Crane, a sketch about a married couple—a quiet, shrewd wife and a loudmouthed husband.

"We can call it 'The Beast,' " suggested Crane.

"Just a second," Gleason replied. "The man isn't a beast at all. The guy really loves this broad. They fight, sure, but they always end in a clinch. . . . I come from a neighborhood full of that stuff. By the time I was fifteen, I knew every insult in the book. . . . But not 'The Beast.' That's not the title."

"How about 'The Lovers'?" Crane offered.

"That's a little closer." Gleason paced the floor. "That could mean that they're not married. We need something that tells everybody at once they're married."

"The Couple Next Door," said Crane.

"No," Gleason countered, a twinkle in his eye, "The Honeymooners."

STEVE ALLEN

He wasn't Berle and he wasn't Benny. He wore neither a dress nor baggy pants. He didn't run around a stage crying, "Wanna buy a duck?" That's because he was Steve Allen.

Steve rarely relied on jokes, per se. He talked, sometimes he laughed. Most of all, he messed around with a lot of papers on his desk. He ate too—a chicken leg, a salami, some homemade cookies sent in by a fan. For most of his laughs, he relied on his guests. They were his springboard to humor. Once one of them showed up with a few live ducks in a wading pool, so Steve went wading too.

When two old ladies in his *Tonight* show audience kept talking noisily to each other during the performance, Steve turned the problem into a plus. He recalls: "I think the heart of all humor is something going wrong. So I slanted all my talk that night to these two old ladies. I could have had a page throw them out, but instead I made them a part of the show."

Having its origins as far back as 1950 with a program called *Broadway Open House*, Steve's *Tonight* show originated from a legitimate theatre in New York's Broadway district, the Hudson. At the back of the stage, there were two huge metal doors called "elephant doors," which opened out onto the side street. Steve often would open them suddenly, with a camera trained on the doors, and begin interviewing surprised passersby. It was a totally spontaneous move which aptly reflects Steve Allen, the man and his wit.

STAR SEARCH

You will find hidden among the maze of letters the last names of 124 television stars described on these pages. To locate them, simply read forward, backward, up, down, and diagonally. You must always travel in a straight line, and you cannot skip letters. Draw a circle around each title that you discover. Letters are permitted to be used more than once, and words may overlap. You will not use all the letters in the maze.

1. His wasn't the greatest show on earth
2. He was Ethel's other half _____
3. The king of Clearasil from Philadelphia _____
4. The country-western hawker of sausage _____
5. He had his Nellybelle _____
6. The Thomases' maid Louise _____
7. Miss Kitty _____
8. The Boswell of the Bronx _____
9. The colonel of Fort Baxter _____
10. She played Lily's friend Hilda _____
11. The late "Johnny Yuma" _____
12. One of the *Felony Squad* _____
13. The nun and the surfer _____
14. The First Lady of Television _____
15. Fort Apache's youngest recruit _____
16. Sullivan's Billy the Kid _____
17. Producer of his brother-in-law's TV show _____
18. Oz's Cowardly Lion _____
19. Jerry Lester's buxom buddy _____
20. She and Ken Carson played with Moore _____
21. The Baxters' hired help _____
22. Jayne Meadows' husband _____
23. Trixie's favorite friend _____
24. The last Beulah _____
25. This Jeannie has blond hair _____
26. *Match Game*'s announcer _____
27. He crowned criers daily _____
28. She played Ray Milland's wife _____
29. The host of *What's My Line?* _____
30. He was *The Virginian* _____
31. Astaire's TV dance partner _____
32. Fenneman's mentor _____
33. Peggy, Janet, Dianne or Kathy _____
34. David Wayne's wife on *Norby* _____
35. This Hoppy wasn't a rabbit _____
36. Man of many disguises in the wild west _____
37. Danny Thomas's second spouse _____
38. Trapper John of Korea _____
39. Head-shrinker for the astronauts _____
40. Victoria Barkley's lawyer son _____
41. Mr. Peck had a bad girl _____
42. Star of TV's longest-running western
43. Madison High's prize teacher _____
44. A super man _____
45. A menace named Dennis _____
46. Lassie's first master _____
47. Mr. Terrific's government liaison _____
48. Lonesome without Alice _____
49. *Your Show of Shows* star _____
50. The white half of *I Spy* _____
51. She was Daisy Moses, formerly of the Ozarks _____
52. The sing-along impressario _____
53. What's the trouble with father? _____
54. *Four Star Playhouse* Frenchman _____
55. New England's Rodney Harrington _
56. *Ramar of the Jungle* _____
57. Chief of C.O.N.T.R.O.L. _____
58. The Ham Burger that wasn't meat _____
59. Steve Allen's favorite forgetter _____
60. Danny Thomas's first wife _____
61. *Peepers'* stuttering star _____
62. From *Laugh-In* to an Oscar _____
63. Francis, the stagehand _____
64. Harry, Sylvester, or Herbert _____
65. Grandpa Walton _____

98

(continued on page 100)

```
O X E S O F U N T Y R A L C Y S L Y N N
B B E W R E S A R F E H A Y E S E E E I
E M F U L L E R M O R S E M B E N L P E A
A D E A R L E K B R S O S N O O Y D A L
E Y A R F T A R N E S S E A T S T A R S
N V R E O R A A H K O D V S M I T H K E
C A N B M Y E L W A R F E E E V E R S N
E N A R C D O C D A L Y E N R A Y N U N
E C Z A D A M S N D C O R E Y D O D D I
N E R B E R G D E A C O N O T T U H O V
O T A O A B O U S G L B N G S U N G G A
T I N O T L E F L M E A D O W S G N O G
S H N T P A L F O A L I P S R A A P K R
E S A H C K I E V R G L R E T T I G E A
R L M L U E D E N X E E D E S S H E E N
P L L C L O R R I N G Y R E V A N E F T
D O A D P S U L T O O D O N W I E R E T
E S T E E K R O R B B N L B W A G L O O
E B S E N A Y R A S E A C R O A A C O C
R Y D E R O O M M I L L E R D H H I M S
```

STAR SEARCH

66. The latest Ellery Queen _____
67. This Anderson always knew best _____
68. Skipper of the *Minnow* _____
69. The water closet joketeller _____
70. The female star of *It's About Time* _____
71. Eddie Haskell's buddy _____
72. Meet Millie and Consuelo _____
73. Officer Gunther Toody _____
74. He played Silver City's deputy _____
75. Carol Burnett's mentor _____
76. He sold his homestead to O.K. Oil Company _____
77. Stretch Snodgrass _____
78. Mrs. Alex Stone _____
79. Christopher Colt, gun salesman _____
80. Uncle Fultie _____
81. The wife of Judge Bradley J. Stevens _____
82. Hope Emerson and Rickey Kelman were his co-stars _____
83. *East Side/West Side*, he was all around the town _____
84. Hollywood's Jeff Spencer _____
85. The head Mouseketeer _____
86. English professor at Channing U. _____
87. Sky King _____
88. Ralph Malph of Milwaukee _____
89. Doc Galen Adams _____
90. A Box brother's girlfriend _____
91. This Martin Kane had the same name as Chester Gould's hero _____
92. He hosted the infamous *Dotto* _____
93. The animated Hanna's partner _____
94. Colonel Hogan of Stalag 13 _____
95. Random House game player _____
96. The clown's Cuban _____
97. Sullivan's spokeswoman _____
98. Whirlybird Chuck Miller _____
99. Prince of pie-throwing _____
100. Miss America's announcer _____
101. Carl Hyatt of Checkmate, Inc. _____
102. Jaffe's medical replacement _____
103. Rocky Graziano was her comedy foil _____
104. Lucy's landlady _____
105. Madison Avenue's Gordon Hathaway
106. Ranger Corey Stuart _____
107. After Ludden on *College Bowl* _____
108. Title star of *Life With Father* _____
109. Kildare's elder _____
110. The Marquis Chimps' sitcom mama _____
111. Commander of *DD181* on *Convoy* _____
112. He let you lead his band _____
113. The mother on *My Son Jeep* _____
114. The head of Century Studios _____
115. The eldest cast member of *Jamie* _____
116. Detective Meyer Meyer of the *87th Precinct* _____
117. Florian ZaBach's ballerina assistant _____
118. *Laramie's* Jess Harper _____
119. Gene Autry's talkative sidekick _____
120. He pursued a fugitive _____
121. LeBeau of Stalag 13 _____
122. Bilko's girlfriend Joan _____
123. He caught people in the act _____
124. The brains behind *Adam-12* _____

They Had a Past

Milton Berle was a vaudevillian since the age of five. Jim Arness played in "B" movies. Burns and Allen were famous in radio—many television stars began their careers long before the medium was a major entertainment force.

Can you recognize the four TV personalities pictured and "described" below?

1. The actor on the left was one of those two.

2. He played a Hollywood detective.

3. He toted a thirties gun.

4. The actress in the middle played three of the same people.

Down the Tube

Here's an excerpt from an unpublished weekly magazine, *Closed Circuit TV Guide.*

FRIDAY
EVENING

DECEMBER 1, 1978

8:00 **1** **3** TORCH SONG—Comedy
Sparks fly as dimpled Doris Day dons hard hat and asbestos muff for her new role as a shop steward at a welding plant. Fenwick: David Doyle

6 **8** PRETTY PETTY—Drama
Soupy Sales plays Soupy Simpson, a no-nonsense judge in this hard-hitting slice of life set in a small claims court in Cleveland. Tonight: An innocent citizen tries to collect $8.75 from a dry cleaner who ruined his favorite Nehru jacket (60 mins.).

7 **12** HOLLYWOOD PAIRS—Game
Regular panelists Mickey Rooney, Zsa Zsa Gabor, Artie Shaw, and Elizabeth Taylor try to figure out whose spouse is whose.

10 **21** PARAPLEGIC BOWLING—Game

13 SEARCH FOR TOMORROW WITH A GUIDING LIGHT TO FIND THE EDGE OF NIGHT AND LOVE OF LIFE DURING A SECRET STORM AS THE WORLD TURNS—Serial
Janet kills herself when she finds out that Harold has terminal dandruff.

8:30 **1** **3** WHAT'S MY CRIME?—Game
There's laughter and loot afoot as muggers, robbers, and extortionists compete for electric knives, getaway

Cadillacs, and bail money. Bert Parks hosts.

7 **12** POPE SCOPE—Comedy
A lighthearted look at married life in the Vatican or, can an agnostic find happiness being married to a man as preoccupied as the Pope? Pope Kevin: David Soul; Charlotte: Farrah Fawcett-Majors

10 **21** JACQUES COUSTEAU—Documentary
The underwater filmmaker surfaces long enough to do an upbeat study on varicose veins (60 mins.).

13 JOURNEY TO NOWHERE—Adventure
Host Bill Burrud travels to deepest, darkest Africa where he soon discovers that his Bankamericard has been revoked.

9:00 **1** **3** IRS-CAPADES—Drama
Burt Reynolds stars as F. Lee Bully, a swashbuckling barrister who handles nothing but income tax cases. Tonight: Bully defends a professional swimmer who claimed a $41,977 deduction for shoelaces (60 mins.).

6 **8** GAY WAY OF THE WEST—Western
Six limp-wristed wranglers ride this TV trail, a saga that promises to reveal just how close a man can get to his horse (60 mins.).

7 12 BY HOOK OR BY CROOK—
Comedy
A bang-up show starring Shirley Jones
as a musical matchmaking madame.

**10 21 ANOTHER AMERICAN
FAMILY—**Documentary
A sequel to the award-winning "An
American Family," but instead of the
William Louds, an upper-middle-class
family on the brink of breaking up,
this version will feature the loud
Williamses, a welfare family of 27 that
can't afford to break up (60 mins.).

**13 100-PROOF BOTTLE
BANQUETS—**Cooking
Phil Harris calls the chef shots in this
new prime-time gourmet foray.
Tonight Phil prepares corn flakes a la
Jack Daniels.

9:30 7 12 ZERO—Drama
Quinn Martin, that prolific producer
of private eye programs, has developed
the ultimate in offbeat TV detectives.
According to press releases, "Nothing
deters the zealous Zero from his
appointed rounds, not even the fact
that he is deaf, dumb, and blind."
Zero Schwartz: Vince Edwards (60
mins.).

13 LET'S MAKE NICE—Comedy
Insults, threats, and venomous repartee
take over in this thigh-slapping sitcom
featuring two feuding families who
share bathroom privileges in a

Communist boarding house that
straddles the Arab and Israeli border.

10:00 1 3 SMUT RAIDERS—Drama
A dozen likeable old ladies portray a
band of barnstorming vigilantes who
voraciously ransack the bureau
drawers of adolescent boys. Miss
Perkins: Helen Hayes (60 mins.).

6 8 TIME'S UP!—Drama
Eva Gabor plays Eva Garcia, a
fashionable ghetto metermaid, in this
gutsy, Jack Webb-produced cop
show. Tonight: Eva unwittingly
issues a parking ticket to an illegal
alien who claims he's God.

10 21 ETHEL'S DEVILS—Drama
Three handsome blond Adonises
team up to solve international
dilemmas. Tonight: Harry tries to get
the goods on a foreign agent who
stole his hair dryer.

13 IRON CURTAINS—Comedy
At press time, diplomatic
arrangements were being finalized to
permit filming of this series set in a
Communist country. The result is a
side-splitting half hour set in a
Chinese hand laundry in Peking.

Once Upon a Horse

The Western, says one aficionado, "gives the average person, fed up with the Freudian interpretation of everything, a chance to look back nostalgically to a time when life was simple . . ."

Americans, so the TV ratings proved, took a nostalgic look backward on a prodigious scale during the 1958–59 season when television played host to more than twenty-five Westerns, a trend that began in 1955 when *Wyatt Earp* and *Gunsmoke,* two "adult" westerns, rode into the medium.

Here, we present a unique visual tribute to that wonderful year of the Western, 1958.

GUNSMOKE. The most durable of all westerns had its origins in radio. In 1952 Norman Macdonnell and John Meston were trying to create a "non-horse opera" for CBS where everyone would behave more or less as human beings behave in real life. Their script, titled *Jeff Spain,* was promptly rejected by CBS's Harry Ackerman because it was "too different." But several months later, with a gaping hole in the CBS Radio lineup, *Spain* was put into production and retitled *Gunsmoke* (Ackerman's contribution). The show was an immediate success with William Conrad (TV's Cannon) as Marshal Matt Dillon.

A few years later the network decided to transfer the series to TV. The lead role was offered to John Wayne (Conrad was too fat for TV) who turned it down but recommended a young actor he had under personal contract, James Arness.

Gunsmoke went on the air September 10, 1955, as a half-hour series, racking up 156 episodes. It was expanded to an hour format in 1961 after which 356 segments were put on film. The show that critic Jack Gould once called "very professional, workmanlike, routine junk," remains one of CBS's greatest triumphs.

James Arness as Marshal Matt Dillon on CBS's Gunsmoke.

James Garner as Bret Maverick (with guest star Joanna Barnes) on Maverick.

Will Hutchins as Sugarfoot *(shown with Lonie Blackman).*

HAVE GUN, WILL TRAVEL. After a stint as Dr. Konrad Styner on *Medic,* Richard Boone went west. On September 14, 1957, he debuted as Paladin (no first name), the suave gun-for-hire who wore a black outfit and sported a leather holster bearing the silver symbol of a white knight chess piece, on *Have Gun, Will Travel.*

The name Paladin was derived from one of Charlemagne's twelve legendary knights who were paragons of chivalry. Like his namesake, Paladin had a taste for Keats, Chateau Haut-Brion, and Ming china. He also was quite a ladies' man.

A former Confederate cavalry officer, Paladin lived at the swanky Hotel Carlton in San Francisco, passed out calling cards with "Have Gun, Will Travel" printed on them, and had a six-year run on CBS for a total of 225 episodes.

SUGARFOOT. A cowboy designated one grade lower than a tenderfoot is a sugarfoot. On September 17, 1957, 25-year-old Will Hutchins debuted in this ABC western, created by Michael Fessier for Warner Brothers Television.

Sugarfoot, with its lead character, law student Tom Brewster, took place on the Frontier in the 1860s. Executive producer William T. Orr, who devised the show specifically for Hutchins, explained his title character: "Tom Brewster is a gentle fellow with a mild sense of humor and a strong sense of justice, who drifts from town to town in search of employment while he carries on a correspondence course in law. Never looking for trouble, he always seems to find it, along with a pretty girl."

Richard Boone as Paladin on Have Gun, Will Travel.

Steve McQueen was Josh Randall on Wanted: Dead or Alive.

Once Upon a Horse

The western ran three seasons, divided into 69 one-hour segments.

THE RIFLEMAN. "They must have been looking at maybe forty, fifty guys that day," recalls Chuck Connors about an afternoon in 1958. "When I came in, the producer picked up a rifle and heaved it at me across the room. I grabbed it and started to heave it back to him. They wanted to see how I handled a rifle."

Connors, late of the Brooklyn Dodgers and Chicago Cubs baseball teams, played widower-rancher Lucas McCain, father of young Mark, played by Johnny Crawford, both residents of North Fork, New Mexico, in 1888.

McCain was billed as "the fastest man with a .44–40 hair-trigger action [Winchester] rifle," from the first of 168 half-hour episodes which began on September 30, 1958.

A shrewd businessman, the 6'5" Connors owned ten percent of everything connected with the series, "including," as he said, "even the office stationery."

ZORRO. A successful movie serial of the 1920s starring Douglas Fairbanks, Sr., in the dual role of Don Diego de la Vega and Zorro, *Zorro* came to TV via the Walt Disney studios on October 10, 1957.

With Armando Catalano, better known as Guy Williams, in the title TV role, this ABC western was set in Monterey, California, in 1820, and ran two seasons.

Williams won the role because he could actually fence, a talent he learned from his father at the age of seven in New York.

Jock Mahoney and X. Brands on Yancy Derringer.

Guy Williams and Henry Calvin of Zorro.

106

Chuck Connors and Johnny Crawford as Lucas and Mark McCain on The Rifleman.

Pat Conway as Sheriff Clay Hollister on Tombstone Territory.

A Warner Brothers Television publicity shot featuring (l-r) Will Hutchins as Sugarfoot, James Garner as Bret Maverick on Maverick, Wayde Preston as Christopher Colt in Colt .45, and Clint Walker as Cheyenne Bodie on Cheyenne.

Clint Eastwood as Rowdy Yates befriends guest star Bill Travers on a Rawhide episode.

Robert Culp as Texas Ranger Hoby Gilman on Trackdown (Rita Moreno guest-starred).

Nonetheless, Fred Cavens, a veteran Hollywood fencing master (he taught Fairbanks the ropes, too) was assigned to guide Williams in the fencing sequences which were carefully worked out on graph paper first.

ANNIE OAKLEY. The first of the 81 episodes of this series was filmed in April, 1953, under the auspices of Gene Autry's company, Flying A Productions. The series starred 28-year-old Gail Davis as Annie Oakley, who was tapped by Autry for the western role after proving herself in one of his films, *Cow Town.* At first, Autry wanted to depict Annie as a 13- or 14-year-old; in fact, he tested a number of actresses in their mid-teens. He soon abandoned that idea and chose Gail because she could handle guns and a horse with natural ease, although he wanted her to "play it young." Autry made a pilot. "It was pretty terrible," Gail says, "and it didn't sell. So we made a second film in which I played pretty much my own age. That did it."

The series ran seven years on ABC and co-starred Brad Johnson as Annie's boyfriend, Sheriff Lofty Craig, and Jimmy Hawkins as her kid brother, Tagg.

RESTLESS GUN. When John Payne decided to take on the challenge of a TV series in 1957, he had appeared in eighty films, six of them westerns. His show, *Restless Gun,* was a western which premiered on September 23, 1957, on NBC and featured the actor as Vint Bonner, a Civil War veteran. "The character is that of a sympathetic working cowhand, an itinerant

Gail Davis as Annie Oakley.

John Russell as
Marshal Dan Troop in
Lawman.

Robert Taylor hosted
Death Valley Days
after Ronald Reagan quit.

Ward Bond was Seth Adams and Robert
Horton was Flint McCullough on
Wagon Train.

Tom Jeffords was portrayed by John Lupton, on Broken Arrow.

Wayde Preston in Colt .45.

Clayton Moore and Jay Silverheels, The Lone Ranger and Tonto.

Clint Walker as Cheyenne Bodie on Cheyenne.

who spends six months in one town, a year in another, and who is pretty well known as a dependable, nice guy," said Payne. "He has a reputation for being fairly handy with a gun, but he's no gunfighter, and he takes pains to play down this skill as much as possible."

For 77 episodes, Payne served as not only star but also executive producer, writer, and narrator. He owned fifty percent of the program through his Window Glen Productions company.

CHEYENNE. This Warner Brothers saga, based on the 1947 movie starring Arthur Kennedy, saw the light of day in the fall of 1955, as part of *Warner Brothers Presents,* a three-series rotating program for ABC.

As a weekly western, *Cheyenne* premiered September 25, 1956, with Clint Walker (real name: Norman Walker) as an 1860s frontier scout Cheyenne Bodie, a man of Indian descent who was schooled in both white and Cheyenne cultures.

Walker, whose size (6'5", 235 pounds) prompted Cecil B. DeMille to hire him to play a pharoah's bodyguard in *The Ten Commandments,* was the perfect choice for *Cheyenne.*

"I think people like to see a big guy like me get beat up," the star once said. In every episode, the huge cowboy actor was either horsewhipped, slugged, walloped, kicked, or mauled. It was all in a day's work . . . which lasted eight years and 107 episodes.

Hugh O'Brian as Sheriff Wyatt Earp on ABC's The Life and Legend of Wyatt Earp.

Jess Oppenheimer on "I Love Lucy"

Lucy and "Oppy" (as Jess was called by his friends and associates) in happier days.

Born in 1913 and raised in San Francisco, Jess Oppenheimer began his writing career in radio. After Stanford University and a brief tenure in the fur business, Jess struck out for Hollywood to get a job in show business. He landed one in typical Oppenheimer style with the Young & Rubicam advertising agency in 1936 with a starting salary of $125 per week. In the medium, Jess used his talents on the *Packard Hour,* which starred Fred Astaire and Charlie Butterworth; the *Jack Benny Program;* the *Chase and Sanborn* show; *Screen Guild;* Fanny Brice's *Baby Snooks Show;* the *Edgar Bergen Show;* and *My Favorite Husband,* a radio show starring Lucille Ball and Richard Denning which he wrote, directed, and produced. In television, he was responsible for *I Love Lucy;* was a program executive with NBC during the late 1950s; and created and produced *Angel* (1960) and *The Debbie Reynolds Show* (1969). In recent years, Jess has devoted much of his time to inventing, with twenty patents to prove his prowess. He loves golf (is writing a unique book about it), continues to work on special TV projects, and is an incurable gadget freak. He lives with his wife Estelle in Brentwood, California. They have two children— Joanne, who lives on a kibbutz in Israel, and Gregg, an attorney.

ANDREWS: You were the producer and head writer of *I Love Lucy* for five seasons, during which time you masterminded 153 episodes of the classic TV series, sharing the writing credit with Madelyn Pugh and Bob Carroll, Jr. Exactly how did you three concoct an *I Love Lucy* script?

OPPENHEIMER: Our schedule demanded that we write a script every single week because we didn't use any outside writers. It was just Bob and Madelyn and I for four years, and then we added Bob Schiller and Bob Weiskopf. In the beginning, Bob and Madelyn and I would meet every Monday morning in my office, after the cast had read the script for the show being shot that week. We had to be there for that reading just in case there were changes needed. It usually wasn't that much, but if Desi didn't like something, we'd change it, because if he didn't like something, he was incapable of doing it. Or sometimes he just wasn't able to understand things that were a part of our American culture. So once those revisions were out of the way, usually by eleven o'clock in the morning, the three of us would lock ourselves away in my office on the lot and start working.

ANDREWS: Did you come armed with lists of possible story ideas or premises, or did you create the situation on the spot?

OPPENHEIMER: Someone would just say, "Does anybody have any ideas?" Then we'd kick around any available notions, finally latch onto one and start developing it. I think in the five years I was on the show, there might have been three times that we didn't finish the story we started on the same day, because if it had taken two or three days to get and develop an idea, there would have been no way to do the series. Of course, it also helped that we had a three-and-a-half-year backlog of scripts from *My Favorite Husband,* and we used a lot of them. Each one had a good solid basis for a story, whether we used any of the particulars or not. And don't forget, we knew those characters very well. That helps a lot.

ANDREWS: Are you saying it was *easy* writing *Lucy*?

OPPENHEIMER: Not easy, no. But if we got onto an idea like "Never Do Business With Friends" [the Ricardos sell their used washing machine to the Mertzes], it would just go, almost write itself . . . almost. And we weren't *trying* to manufacture something funny, either.

ANDREWS: I always thought that you started with a funny comedy bit for the end and worked backwards to build up to it.

OPPENHEIMER: If someone asked me the difference between *I Love Lucy* and Lucy's subsequent series [*The Lucy Show* and *Here's Lucy*], I would have to say that we started with an *idea* and developed it into a *story,* whereas they probably started with a big physical comedy concept for the end, and worked backwards, *trying* to make a story out of it, and that's just impossible, as far as I'm concerned. I always insisted that everything in an *I Love Lucy* story have a logical foundation. I wanted there to be a sound reason for everything in the script, because I knew from experience that if you take viewers one step at a time, and they know *why*

they're being taken there, you can go to the heights of slapstick comedy and outlandish situations. An audience lives in a cause-and-effect world: nothing happens without a reason and you cannot give them things that don't make sense.

ANDREWS: That sounds like a lot of work.

OPPENHEIMER: It was. We would spend many hours on that Monday taking all the information necessary to the plot and lacing it into the story while other things were happening so it would flow naturally. We usually worked on this outlining until five o'clock, but sometimes until seven. We'd just kick the story back and forth, and, when we finally felt we had it, I'd dictate the entire thing into a machine while it was fresh. In fact, we'd often get other ideas when we heard it being talked aloud. By the next morning, we all had a typed draft of that outline. Then Bob and Madelyn would go off on their own and write a first draft which they would deliver to me two days later, on Wednesday night. I'd go over it carefully on Thursday, amid my other responsibilities on the show, and return it to them with comments and suggestions for changes, and they'd give me another draft by the following Monday when we'd all sit down again to work on a new script. At that point, the script never went back to them. I'd do a "polish" (rewrite it) and would redictate the entire script from start to finish into my dictation machine.

ANDREWS: What if their draft was perfect as is?

OPPENHEIMER: I made it a point, no matter

how good their draft was, to redictate the entire thing, from beginning to end, because that way each of the characters consistently spoke the same way. It didn't have to be *me,* necessarily, but as long as it was filtered through one person's senses . . . There was another reason for this. The fact that I knew every aspect of every script meant that if a question arose at any time during the production of that episode, I knew the reason why something was in there—a line, a piece of business, whatever. So if they wanted to make a change, I would immediately know if we couldn't do it because of something that preceded the proposed change. There has to be one person with that sort of overview. I remember one time that Bob and Madelyn gave me their draft and I felt it was *so* good, and I was so tired, that I said, "That's just the way I would do it; I'm going to turn it into mimeograph without any changes." So at the first reading with the actors, questions naturally arose and I was completely lost because I didn't have any of the answers. I had no idea why a certain line was in there, or a bit of business. It scared me half to death, and I never did it again.

ANDREWS: What were Bob and Madelyn's feelings about your "tampering" with their scripted brainchildren?

OPPENHEIMER: Even though we always got along great, they thought I loused up all their scripts. One time, after they complained bitterly to me, I said, "There's a good and logical reason for everything I do, everything I change. So,

From 1947 to 1951, Jess Oppenheimer produced, wrote, and directed CBS Radio's My Favorite Husband *series which starred Lucy and Richard Denning (later star of* Mr. and Mrs. North *on TV).*

on the next script, I'm going to keep a journal of all my changes and the reasons why." I told them, "Now you're going to know why I make alterations." So I did it, and it took a lot of time, but I felt it was worth it. The next time we sat down to talk, I asked them if they had read my revision. Figuring that I had done a pretty masterful job, I told them that I would show them line by line the reasons for every change. Frankly, I thought they would throw themselves at my feet when I finished. But when I got through, I asked them whether they agreed. They

A scene from "Lucy Is Envious," one of Jess Oppenheimer's least favorite Lucy *episodes.*

The I Love Lucy *writers spent hours making sure this classic candy-factory sequence from "Job Switching" was logical. Logical or not, it was one of the funniest moments in television history.*

said, "No. We still think you screwed up the whole thing."

ANDREWS: Could you go into a little more detail about how you *logically* worked the comedy into a *Lucy* script?

OPPENHEIMER: Let's take the candy factory scene ["Job Switching"]. You've probably seen this bit fifty or sixty times on other shows. It's a very old concept, the assembly-line. But I don't think I've ever seen another show that didn't violate the logic of the moment. They'd have the conveyor belt speeding up and slowing down just for comedic effect, but without regard to logic. And that's the kind of thing that turns off an audience. It suddenly reminds them that this is just for fun, rather than allowing them to be comfortable and go with it. Even that bread scene in "Pioneer Women" is a logical extension of what *could* happen if one put in too much yeast. And "The Freezer" episode—it was merely an imaginative extension, having her come out with icicles on her face. It's not *completely* illogical. But had we had her come out of the freezer frozen in a giant block of ice, then we would have lost everyone. Don't forget, we didn't always *try* to get the laugh. We took time to develop a situation that would eventually pay off with a bigger laugh.

ANDREWS: Somehow, I always thought that with a show like "Lucy's Italian Movie," where Lucy winds up in a huge vat of wine grapes, you must have started your brainstorming session with the statement, "Let's do a show where Lucy winds up in a vat of grapes."

Every nuance and bit of business was carefully written into an I Love Lucy *script, including the Vitameatavegamin scene from "Lucy Does a TV Commercial," originally telecast May 5, 1952.*

OPPENHEIMER: Absolutely not. It was a logical development of the basic premise. We knew that the Ricardos and Mertzes were going through Italy. Then Bob and Madelyn and I got to talking about Italian movies—how earthy they were— and we thought it might be funny to have Lucy be in one. But, of course, how do we get her into an Italian movie? Then we got the idea that an Italian movie producer sees her on the train; he offers her a role. Then we had to figure out how Lucy could get in the "mood" for an Italian movie role, get some experience. I think there was a discussion about winemaking. Then one of us suggested it would be funny if Lucy were stomping grapes with her feet. I remember we had a large problem with the fact that she'd be unable to understand Italian, and vice versa, and we made a couple of attempts based on her inability to understand, but then we decided to use the subtitles. Then we thought about those things which are stereotypically Italian and tried to work them in. I recall one thing we wrote which Lucy couldn't do. She was standing barefoot on the hot pavement and she couldn't do the natural thing of standing on one foot as long as you can stand it, then switching over to the other foot and hopping back and forth. She tried the bit, but couldn't cut it, which was very unusual for her. She always did everything we wrote, without question. In fact, let me read that section of the script to you:

WE FADE IN ON A GRAPE VINEYARD. THERE'S A LITTLE CLEARING WITH COBBLESTONES AND PERHAPS A WELL. IN THE BACKGROUND THERE ARE THE VINEYARDS. NEARBY IS A LARGE WINE VAT FOR GRAPE-PRESSING. THE SIDES ARE KNEE-HIGH. SEVERAL ITALIAN WOMEN IN NATIVE GARB AND BAREFOOT ARE STANDING IN GROUPS WAITING FOR THE FOREMAN TO HIRE THEM. AT TIMES DURING THE FOLLOWING, TWO MALE WORKERS APPROACH THE VAT, EMPTYING BUSHEL BASKETS OF GRAPES INTO IT. IT'S PRETTY FULL.

Incidentally, I remember a big problem we had was with Lucy's hair. We knew she'd wind up under the water and, because her hair was very susceptible to dye, they had to find something that wasn't going to leave her with purple hair. They finally came up with a food coloring. Even the wine industry, who got wind of the episode, got into the act. They insisted we put in something about the fact that wine wasn't made this primitive way anymore. So we had a bellboy at the Ricardos' Rome hotel say something about this place in Turo being the only place where it's still done the old-fashioned way. But, anyway, to go back to the script:

LUCY FOLLOWS HER INTO THE VAT. LUCY LOOKS OVER THE EDGE AND SEES WHAT SHE'S DOING AND LOOKS SQUEAMISH. THE WOMAN INDICATES WITH A WAVE OF HER ARM TO COME ON. LUCY CAUTIOUSLY CLIMBS IN AND GINGERLY PUTS HER FOOT ON THE GRAPES. HER FACE REFLECTS THAT THIS IS A VERY WEIRD SENSATION. THE ITALIAN WOMAN IS STOMPING VIGOROUSLY, AND LUCY LOOKS LIKE SHE IS WALKING ON EGGS. THE WOMAN REACTS TO LUCY'S DELICATE AIR, STOPS AND ILLUSTRATES FOR LUCY BY STOMPING HARD. LUCY, GETTING THE IDEA, GOES AT IT WITH FULLER ENTHUSIASM, LIKE A RUNNER RUNNING IN PLACE. SHE BEGINS TO ENJOY THIS, AND STARTS RUNNING AROUND THE VAT, THEN TRIES TRICK STEPS LIKE A BALLET DANCER OR PERHAPS LIKE A PERSON WITH ONE LEG SHORTER THAN THE OTHER, ETC. LUCY REACHES UP TO CHECK HER EARRING WHICH IS LOOSE, TIGHTENS IT, THEN CHECKS THE OTHER EAR AND FINDS THAT HER EARRING IS MISSING. SHE LOOKS ALARMED AND REALIZES IT'S DOWN IN THE GRAPES. SHE STARTS FEELING AROUND WITH ONE FOOT TRYING TO FIND THE EARRING. THE OTHER WOMAN NOTICES THAT SHE ISN'T WORKING, COMES OVER AND NUDGES HER AND INDICATES THAT SHE SHOULD KEEP STOMPING. THE WOMAN STARTS STOMPING TO SHOW LUCY. SHE SUDDENLY GETS A PAINED EXPRESSION AS SHE STEPS ON THE EARRING. SHE HOPS UP AND DOWN HOLDING HER FOOT. LUCY QUICKLY TAKES OFF THE OTHER EARRING AND THROWS IT AWAY. SHE STARTS STOMPING AWAY AS WE FADE OUT.

ANDREWS: That's not the same scene we see

The grape vat scene from "Lucy's Italian Movie." Teresa Tirelli battles it out with Lucille Ball, filmed in early 1956.

on TV, is it? There was nothing about earrings.

OPPENHEIMER: What was actually done—Lucy getting tired after all the fooling around in the vat, then having a fight with the other woman—was probably developed on the set during rehearsals. I can't recall at what point that new business was created. It may have been that Bob and Madelyn and I saw the first dress rehearsal and felt the scene needed more, that it didn't quite build up to a big enough height, comedically, or it may have been that the actors just improvised that wonderfully marvelous scene. The actors were absolutely free to do whatever they wanted and then if I came down to the stage and agreed, it stayed in. If I didn't agree, then we had a long discussion about it.

ANDREWS: How important were discussions of this nature?

OPPENHEIMER: We had two such sessions for every show. One was a run-through on Tuesday night where the actors tried to put down their scripts for the first time. This would give me a good idea as to what was working and what wasn't. Then we had a "note session" where

we'd discuss everything that I made notes on. I'd give my suggestions about readings, or whatever wasn't working. The next evening, there would be a second run-through, a first dress rehearsal, at about five o'clock. It would be over by 6:30, and then we'd bring in sandwiches and have another note session. Everyone stayed for this, even stagehands, and we were rarely out of there before eleven or 11:30. They were wonderful sessions where we'd even get into the philosophy of the script. We'd have our share of arguments too. Bill Frawley would get his back up over the way he wanted to read a line or something. But they were very stimulating and fruitful. We really dug into the characters because we took these people very seriously and tried to make

Jess's 41st birthday party in late 1954. This photo, taken in his studio office on Cahuenga Boulevard in Hollywood, features Oppenheimer's wife, Estelle.

Jess Oppenheimer.

Jess with (l−r) Desi Arnaz, Terry Clyne (Philip Morris ad agency representative), Madelyn Pugh (co-writer), Bob Carroll, Jr. (co-writer), and Lucy.

everything logical. There's that word again.

ANDREWS: Is it true that very little of *I Love Lucy* was actually ad-libbed?

OPPENHEIMER: Basically, Lucy is not a funny person. However, she could come up with things that were remarkable. For instance, there was a scene in "Lucy in the Swiss Alps," where she is gingerly picking up crumbs from her sandwich. Just a little moment, but it was truly inspired and it was all Lucy's. She was good about her own character; she had the ability to throw in little, universally humorous things. She was right on the taproots of humanness.

ANDREWS: The *I Love Lucy* reruns are broadcast twice a day in Los Angeles. How often do *you* watch them?

OPPENHEIMER: I don't watch very often. I used to remember every incident that happened during rehearsals, but now it's got to the point where I don't even recall how a story ends, let alone details. My son Gregg and his wife watch them quite a bit and they call me up and complain about what scenes have been cut. Or they'll call to find out how something

turns out, but I can't remember. Not too long ago, a young clerk at Sears recognized my name from my charge plate. That was fun.

ANDREWS: Did *I Love Lucy* make you a wealthy man?

OPPENHEIMER: My contract called for a percentage of the show in perpetuity. Besides the money I earned while I was working on the show as producer and head writer [1951–1956], I've earned a handsome amount of money . . . for not doing anything. I also received another large chunk of money by settling a lawsuit out of court in 1974. My contract called for a royalty to me if the Lucy character was used on another show. Lucy Carmichael and Lucy Carter were merely extensions of Lucy Ricardo, the character I helped create. They tried their hardest *not* to have to pay me, but in the end, just as we were about to start the trial, they made a settlement.

ANDREWS: How did Lucille Ball react to that?

OPPENHEIMER: From the day I filed the lawsuit, I ceased to exist in her mind. Whenever she praises her writers in an interview, my name is never mentioned. It's as if I never had anything to do with *I Love Lucy*.

ANDREWS: I love *what*??

118

MISSING PERSONS

Can you identify the unidentified actors from the clues provided?

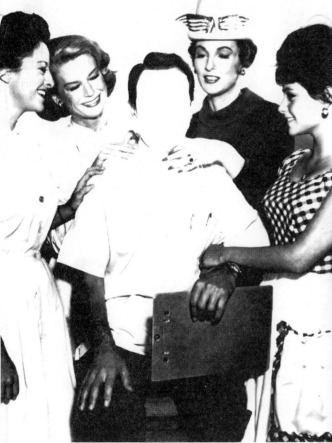

1. Dr. Steve Hardy.

2. DD180's Commander Dan Talbot.

4. *Rex Randolph, private investigator in New Orleans.*

3. *Mayberry's fix-it man.*

5. *Del Stark, Marshal Frank Regan's deputy on* The Dakotas.

6. *Rob Petrie and Sally Rogers' fictional TV employer.*

7. *Sock Miller's girlfriend.*

8. *Movie star Mona Jackson married Mike McCluskey.*

10. *John Monroe, the cartoonist for Manhattanite magazine.*

9. *The song-and-dance dynamo of* Washington Square.

Series Search

You will find hidden among the maze of letters the eighty-one television programs described on these pages. To locate them, simply read forward, backward, up, down, and diagonally. You must always travel in a straight line, and you cannot skip letters. Draw a circle around each title that you discover. Letters are permitted to be used more than once, and words may overlap. You will not use all the letters in the maze.

1. Kingfish and company

2. Lawford writes of love

3. Seth, Flint, and Charlie on the trail

4. Not the famous baby doctor

5. Tales by real-life reporters

6. Animated family life in the 21st Century

7. Earl J. Waggedorn's friend's mama

8. Frank Gallop hosts the rehashed radio show

9. Sherwood Forest, TV-style

10. Dave mugs with J. Fred

11. Henrietta hasn't a ghost of a chance

12. Wendell Corey shrinks heads

13. On the Garrett Ranch

14. Mr. and Mrs. Richard Benjamin

15. Korean War for laughs

16. Joe and his secretary Peggy

17. Dr. Konrad Styner

18. Press agentry on the Great White Way

19. Larry Harmon clowns

20. The bucolic *Laugh-In*

21. Nick Adams after the Civil War

22. Suave and wealthy, Mr. Milland

23. A depot at Sunrise, Colorado

24. Lee is granted a divorce

25. Scott, the tennis pro

26. Henry Mancini, Hope Emerson, and Lola

27. Rory Calhoun in the 1870s

28. This Casey Jones was not Alan Hale

29. Coca cleans up

30. The quiz scandals began here

31. Pahoo-Ka-Ta-Wah

32. Pat Garrett and Billy the Kid

33. Kathryn Forbes and her bank account

34. Two boys and a pachyderm

35. Hector and his Puerto Rican "pups"

36. Rangers Three: Reese, Chad, and Joe

37. After the *Empire* is over

38. "Give that man twenty silver dollars"

39. Dan Adams, private eye

40. A Philadelphia lawyer by Carey

41. The college drop-in

42. Ex-captain Layne

43. Boston kids put on a show

44. Jonathan Drake was trapped in this one

45. How, Burt Reynolds?

46. Coca Cola twice-a-week

47. Florida in Chicago

```
B T E G D I G B L I C O D M L K W A H I
E N A H S C O K E T I M E O O C N O R B
U E E I D N O L B L R E C O R O N A D O
L C B D A F D O D E E K O Z E E L E H M
A C I N U P T N D N U V Y O P L B E W A
H A Z E L A I I J P I R E O P E O E D H
C A N N O N M N E U O R P N O L Z O L K
R L A S S I E O T T L I G H T S O U T R
E M E E T C S B S A S I P W A H E E H A
G L O E I W A G O N T R A I N O H S A M
N E K D N M I N N G A E R I P M E O A R
A U G U S B A S S E R N B F C E A N U B
D R O C P I R J D L T O D A Y I N O U R
N T N E A T W O A D R T P Y S I D S N O
A A E I C N N U G R E T E P X E S E A A
M D O N E R G O R I K O Y R R T H A M D
T O N I G H T E A Q D D T A O M E A L W
A H I D I A N A N C Y E L P R A M X L A
B R E N N E R E G N I R R E D Y C N A Y
D A D A U Q S D O M L R I G T A H T T N
```

48. A horse is a horse?

49. Ezio's brood

50. Chic Young's come to life

51. With and without Pernell

52. Dr. Barnard Hughes

53. A liberal beehive

54. Booth-to-Burke

55. Jeff's collie

56. The Robinsons without a map

57. A poet named Ciardi

58. French Annie

59. "Verrrrry interesting"

60. Don Hollinger's girl

61. Tim Conway in cowboy boots

62. The police web

63. They rigged a comedy for her

64. Long-haired cops

65. The professor's surfing daughter

66. An orphan in deWilde

67. Westbrook Van Voorhis scares me

68. Chubby shamus

69. Arlene Francis between *Today* and *Tonight*

70. The President's daughter

71. Sky-diving made easy

72. Zenlee, the champ

73. Elder wise men

74. Allen Carson Paar

75. Father and Son and the Confidential Squad

76. Gotham City's finest

77. New York-to-Minneapolis-to-New York

78. The nouveau executive

79. Dick Starks gets "murdered"

80. The Hendersons' hired help

81. David Carradine never came back

Behind-the-Scenes
at the TV Sitcoms

Morey Amsterdam (Buddy Sorrell) and Rose Marie (Sally Rogers) conduct the "warm up" for the studio audience assembled at Desilu Studios for a filming of CBS's The Dick Van Dyke Show.

Socialite turned actress, Jane Wyatt, relaxes on the Father Knows Best *set at Screen Gems as she studies script.*

Fred DeCordova (right) confers with George Burns and Gracie Allen on the set of the team's sitcom filmed at General Service Studios in Hollywood. Fred now produces Johnny Carson's Tonight Show.

Gale Storm pauses between takes at the Hal Roach Studio set of My Little Margie *during summer 1953 in anticipation of the series debut on NBC-TV.* Margie *began as the 1952 summer replacement for* I Love Lucy *on CBS.*

Stars Lucille Ball and Desi Arnaz pose with Madelyn Pugh, Bob Carroll, Jr., and Jess Oppenheimer, the three most important people in the I Love Lucy success story. The three writers took Lucy from My Favorite Husband *and created the milestone TV situation comedy which has been the basis for countless sitcoms that followed.*

My Friend Irma *starred Marie Wilson (far right) as the scatter-brained secretary. Here, Donald MacBride, Sid Tomack, and Cathy Lewis do a run-through for the cameras. The show was the first program to be made at the newly built (1951) CBS Television City in Hollywood.*

The Donna Reed Show *celebrates its 100th program with a cake-cutting ceremony after a day's shooting. Paul Petersen, who played Jeff Stone, leans on the stagelight, Donna presides over the cake, flanked by Carl Betz and Shelley Fabares who played Alex and Mary Stone, her husband and daughter.*

Don Knotts, Andy Griffith, and Jim Nabors pose on the Mayberry sttreet set at Desilu-Culver (once The Selznick Studios where Gone With the Wind *was filmed). The show ran eight years on CBS and made Griffith a millionaire.*

The Way We Weren't

Will the good old days of television ever return? It's not likely. But did you ever wonder what today's shows would be like if they had been on in the 1950s, and what the 1950s shows would be like if they were on the air today?

THE WAY IT WAS THEN

6 8 OZZIE AND HARRIET—*Comedy*
Ozzie does his best to help Harriet when she becomes editor of the Women's Club News. But his idea for a gossip item does more harm than good.

2 4 DRAGNET—*Drama*
Friday and Smith are assigned to cover the theft of a necktie manufacturer's valuable inventory.

5 9 PRIVATE SECRETARY—*Comedy*
Susie throws the entire office into an uproar when she invests all her savings in some uranium stock.

3 13 MEDIC—*Drama*
A nineteen-year-old girl finds herself about to become a mother.

7 10 PEOPLE ARE FUNNY—*Game*
Art Linkletter sends out a six-year-old girl with an ice cream cone. The little girl is to drop the ice cream on the sidewalk to see if anyone will take pity and buy her another.

11 12 I MARRIED JOAN—*Comedy*
Judge Stevens is called on to decide the custody of a chimpanzee who has inherited a great deal of money from an animal lover.

22 52 BIG TOWN—*Drama*
A high school principal's job is threatened when an expelled youngster decides to "get even."

THE WAY IT WOULD BE NOW

6 8 OZZIE AND HARRIET—*Comedy*
Ozzie does his best to help Harriet when she becomes head of the local Women's Lib movement. But his idea for a "burn-your-bra" day does more harm than good, especially to the overweight members.

2 4 DRAGNET—*Drama*
Friday and Smith are assigned to cover the theft of a heroin manufacturer's valuable inventory.

5 9 PRIVATE SECRETARY—*Comedy*
Susie throws the entire office into an uproar when she announces that the office boy got her pregnant.

3 13 MEDIC—*Drama*
A nineteen-year-old girl finds herself about to become a schizophrenic.

7 10 PEOPLE ARE FUNNY—*Game*
Art Linkletter sends out a six-year-old girl with a joint. The little girl is to drop the reefer on the sidewalk to see if anyone will take pity and sell her another.

11 12 I MARRIED JOAN—*Comedy*
Judge Stevens is called on to decide the custody of a ten-year-old homosexual who has inherited a great deal of money from an interior decorator.

22 52 BIG TOWN—*Drama*
A high school principal's life is threatened when an expelled youngster kidnaps him and holds him for an unusual ransom—an "A" in deportment.

THE WAY IT IS NOW

6 8 JAMES AT 16—*Drama*
James fears that his encounter with a Swedish exchange student has left him with VD.

2 4 SOAP—*Comedy*
Burt and Mary nervously prepare for their first lovemaking attempt in six months. Also, Jodie decides he no longer wants a sex-change operation.

5 9 EXECUTIVE SUITE—*Drama*
An interracial love affair that breaks all the rules risks breaking one more. Summer decides whether to keep Brian's baby or have an abortion.

3 13 BARNABY JONES—*Drama*
A young nun is suspected of pulling the plug on the life-support machine of her terminally-ill sister, a fashion model who was injured in a mysterious accident.

7 10 POLICE WOMAN—*Drama*
Pepper poses as a prostitute to learn why an attempt was made on the life of the new chief of police.

11 12 ALL IN THE FAMILY—*Comedy*
The struggling Stivics feel forced to adopt more effective birth-control methods after Gloria discovers she might be pregnant again.

22 52 PHYLLIS—*Comedy*
Bess is hiding her pregnancy from Mark who has run away because he feels inadequate as a husband and provider.

THE WAY IT WOULD HAVE BEEN THEN

6 8 JAMES AT 16—*Drama*
James worries about his date with a Swedish exchange student—she's three inches taller than him.

2 4 SOAP—*Comedy*
Burt and Mary nervously prepare for their first picnic in six months. Also, Jodie decides he no longer wants his hot rod.

5 9 EXECUTIVE SUITE—*Drama*
Summer's romance with a Protestant breaks all the rules, but the big question is whether to have a May or June wedding.

3 13 BARNABY JONES—*Drama*
A young nun gets into trouble when she takes away the bottle of aspirin from her headachy sister, a Girl Scout leader who has a noisy troop.

7 10 POLICE WOMAN—*Drama*
Pepper masquerades as a metermaid to nab an out-of-state driver who's been parking overnight in a one-hour zone.

11 12 ALL IN THE FAMILY—*Comedy*
The struggling Stivics feel forced to adopt more effective money management methods after Gloria discovers she might be spending more than her budget allows.

22 52 PHYLLIS—*Comedy*
Bess is hiding the present she bought for Mark's birthday because she feels it's inadequate.

Pros, Not Cons

This test concerns TV's portrayal of professionals: lawyers, nurses, entertainers, newspaper reporters, teachers, and doctors. No sheepskin required, just a keen memory.

LAWYERS

1. Who played Owen Marshall's assistant Jess Brandon?_____

2. Where was *Judd for the Defense* set? _____

3. Who was Perry Mason's receptionist? _____

4. Who portrayed San Francisco attorney Sam Benedict?_____

5. Name the father-and-son lawyer team on *The Defenders.* _____

NURSES

Match the nurse character with the actress who portrayed her and name the series.

1. Nurse Chambers _____

2. Liz Thorpe _____

3. Dixie McCall _____

4. Consuelo Lopez _____

5. Nurse Hubbell_____

a. Jayne Meadows

b. Mary Fickett

c. Elena Verdugo

d. Julie London

e. Frances Beers

ENTERTAINERS

1. What was Eve's stage name on *Mr. Adams and Eve?* _____

2. At what nightclub did Danny Williams perform?_____

3. *Bracken's World* was set at what movie studio? _____

4. What theatrical agency handled Ann Marie on *That Girl?* _____

5. Name the character Dick Preston portrayed on the fictional soap opera *Those Who Care.* __

NEWSPAPERMEN

Match the reporter with the newspaper on which he worked, and name the show.

1. Bob Major _____

2. Lou Grant_____

3. Danny Taylor _____

4. Steve Wilson _____

5. Jim Thompson_____

a. *New York Globe*

b. *Phippsboro Bulletin*

c. *Los Angeles Sun*

d. *Los Angeles Tribune*

e. *Illustrated Press*

Pros, Not Cons

TEACHERS

Match the teacher with the school where he or she taught, and name the series.

1. John Novak _____
2. Alice Johnson _____
3. Lucas Tanner _____
4. Miss Landers _____
5. Harvey Weskitt _____
6. Connie Brooks _____

a. Jefferson High School

b. Truman Memorial High School

c. Grant Avenue Grammar School

d. Madison High School

e. Jefferson Junior High School

f. Walt Whitman High School

DOCTORS

Match the doctor with the hospital where he practiced, and name the series.

1. Steve Hardy _____
2. David Zorba _____
3. Paul Mercy _____
4. Matt Powers _____
5. Leonard Gillespie _____
6. Peter Goldstone _____
7. Jake Goodwin _____

a. County General Hospital

b. New North Hospital

c. General Hospital

d. Lowell Memorial Hospital

e. Blair General Hospital

f. Capitol General Hospital

g. Hope Memorial Hospital

TREKKIE FEVER

It's September, 1966. The National Broadcasting Company unleashes its seasonal cache of new TV shows, ballyhooing them as "the greatest premiere attractions in television history." Great attractions like *Hey, Landlord, The Roger Miller Show, The Monkees, The Road West, Occasional Wife, The Girl from U.N.C.L.E., Tarzan, The Hero, T.H.E. Cat,* and, of course, *Star Trek.*

The peacock-symbol network gives the hour-long science fiction series its Thursday-at-8:30 P.M. slot, tenuously sandwiched between *Daniel Boone* (in its third season) and *The Hero* (a new sitcom from the producers of *Get Smart!* that will fade by midseason), and up against CBS's formidable *My Three Sons* (in its seventh, motherless year) and the *Thursday Night Movie,* and ABC's *Tammy Grimes Show* (one of TV's biggest disasters) and *Bewitched* (one of TV's biggest hits).

Despite these programming difficulties, *Star Trek* somehow found its audience—an unbelievably loyal bunch—and remained on the air three seasons, making it NBC's longest-running new series that premiered that year. Its ratings were never spectacular and, in fact, the show was on the verge of cancellation after its second year. Five hundred Cal. Tech. students showed up at NBC's Burbank headquarters and led a vociferous protest march; every science fiction magazine in existence launched wide-reaching campaigns to stop the cancellation. Canadian fans in British Columbia even took out and paid for newspaper ads proclaiming, "Unite to Save the Show." In a week's time, 16,000 letters of protest had arrived at NBC executive offices, and by the end of three months, one million expressions of disappointment—not to mention outright horror—had been tallied by network statisticians. The result, of course, was that *Star Trek* was saved, for another year.

The show ended its network run on June 3, 1969, with the telecast of "Turnabout Intruder." But ten years or so later, the seventy-eight existing color episodes are still running in syndication in over 150 domestic TV markets and in a large number of foreign countries, a tribute to *Star Trek*'s loyal followers. This faithful cult of fans, who have become known as Trekkies (they don't like the label), became the major force in keeping the show, and its boundless spirit, alive.

To term the "movement" a mere phenomenon would be an injustice. When the first "official" *Star Trek* convention took place in 1972 at New York's aging Commodore Hotel, a handful of fans was expected to attend. What happened? Thirty-five hundred card-carrying Trekkies showed up and there was bedlam. A year later, 7,000 people showed up, each playing five dollars admission, and more had to be turned away at the door. They came from all over the world to mingle with their overzealous peers and exchange such dubious curiosities as "authentic" Vulcan pendants and pointed ears made of Latex.

Just how well do you recall the show? Here are twenty questions to test you for the post of honorary crew member on the *Enterprise.*

1. Where were the main components of the *Enterprise* assembled?

2. What connection, if any, did Lucille Ball have with *Star Trek?*

3. Can you name Jim Kirk's deceased brother?

4. On what deck of the spaceship was Dr. McCoy's medical lab located?

5. What Enterprise crew member had green blood?

6. What were the three principal operating divisions to which crew members were assigned?

7. What was Spock's father's name?

8. Name the very first *Star Trek* episode.

9. How long was the *Enterprise*'s original mission supposed to last, according to the opening narration?

10. Gene Roddenberry's daughter Dawn appeared in what *Star Trek* episode?

11. What was Chekov's first name?

12. What type of conditions will qualify a Class M planet?

13. What were the first four words of the opening narration?

14. Who was the first crewman to acquire a tribble?

15. In Vulcan language, what does "Kroykah" mean?

16. How many stars appear on The United Federation of Planets' flag?

17. What was Leo Francis Walsh's real name?

18. Who was captain of the S.S. *Beagle*?

19. What was a tricorder?

20. Who was the chief engineer of the *Enterprise*?

WHAT'S IN A NAME?

Lucille Ball was born Lucille Ball. Ozzie Nelson's real name is Ozzie Nelson. However, there are hundreds of television stars whose real names are remnants of the past. Below are the actual names of twenty TV personalities, accompanied in each case by one of their TV series. How many can you identify?

1. Peggy Middleton in *The Munsters*

2. Ruby Stevens in *The Big Valley*

3. Donald Yarmy in *The Partners*

4. Jack Ryan in *Stoney Burke*

5. Roy Fitzgerald in *McMillan and Wife*

6. Bernie Schwartz in *The Persuaders*

7. Margone Chandler in *Your Hit Parade*

8. Amos Jacobs in *The Practice*

9. Barbara Brantingham in *Mr. and Mrs. North*

10. Mervyn Bogue in *The College of Musical Knowledge*

11. Patricia Neal in *The New Dick Van Dyke Show*

12. Donna Mae Jaden in *It's Always Jan*

13. Josephine Cottle in *Oh! Susanna*

14. Murray Janowsky in *Dollar a Second*

15. George Letz in *Cimarron City*

16. Spangler Brough in *Death Valley Days*

17. Charles Aldrich in *Our Miss Brooks*

18. Aaron Chwatt in *The Double Life of Henry Phyfe*

19. Reginald Truscott-James in *Meet Mr. McNulty*

20. Gail Shikles in *Mr. Broadway*

Recollections of a TV Addict

It was on August 8, 1950, that dear old dad brought home our first television set. I remember it well . . . a 12-inch RCA Victor, Model T-120, Serial Number C1800047 (when I remember, I *remember*). But what do I *really* recall about my twenty-eight years of television viewing? Come back with me now to those thrilling days of yesteryear. The lone(ly) TV addict rides again!

1950: I remember Groucho Marx sparring with dimwitted *You Bet Your Life* contestants. . . . Faye Emerson's cleavage (some dust collector) . . . Superman and his X-ray vision, which I thought would have been a terrific talent on a crowded school bus . . . the little gold heart necklace on Arlene Francis, one of the panelists on *What's My Line?* . . . a boring show called *Your Hit Parade,* where the likes of Snooky Lanson and Dorothy Collins sang the same songs *ad nauseum* . . . my favorite chubby, Kate Smith, whose moons went over one too many mountains.

1951: I remember Edward R. Murrow and his *See It Now* program. . . . Amos, Andy, the Kingfish, Sapphire, and, especially, Lightnin' on *Amos 'n' Andy* (I haven't seen it in nearly twenty years) . . . *Racket Squad* with Captain Braddock and that familiar word of his, "bunco" . . . the beginning of my all-time favorite show, *I Love Lucy* . . . an "insane" man, Ernie Kovacs whom I loved dearly until his untimely death in 1962 . . . the little fellow with "a checkered coat and a funny giggle in his throat," Pinky "The Lisp" Lee . . . a really tasteless show called *Strike It Rich* where blind, deaf, and deformed people vied for prizes.

1952: I remember *Dragnet* with Sergeant Joe Friday and his partner, Frank Smith, and that grimy hand at the end of the show. Talk about dumb-de-dumb-dumb. . . . a show I still watch every morning, *Today* . . . celebrities being surprised by Ralph Edwards; I cried a lot during *This Is Your Life* . . . I would have watched Fulton J. Sheen on Tuesday night but I had to go to bed early. . . . Liberace was always a thrill-and-a-half. . . . a fun game show called *I've Got a Secret* with Garry Moore; I used to look away when they flashed the answer on the screen, so I could play along with Henry Morgan, Betsy Palmer, and Bess Myerson.

1953: I remember *Marty* (thought I was gonna say Mama, right?) and especially how boring life must have been in the Bronx if you were a butcher. . . . Danny Williams and wise-cracking Rusty. . . . Red

Recollections of a TV Addict

Skelton and his many funnymen: Freddie the Freeloader, Clem Kadiddlehopper, Cauliflower McPugg, Willy Lump Lump, and more . . . Little Ricky was born on *I Love Lucy* . . . my first look at Ralph Kramden and Ed Norton on Gleason's variety show . . . Herbert Philbrick, better known as Richard Carlson, in *I Led Three Lives* (I didn't even know what Communism was).

1954: I remember Miss America, on TV for the first time; she was 37-24-36 and from Ephrata, Pennsylvania. . . . Senator Joseph McCarthy of Wisconsin, not so much for what he had done, but for what he was doing to television, preempting Robert Q. Lewis . . . Lassie and his little friend, Jeff, whom I secretly wanted to be . . . Betty Furness opening refrigerator doors (what a talent) . . . Ray Milland playing a college professor . . . Sammy Kaye giving everyone a chance to lead his band . . . Rin Tin Tin and his buddy Rusty of B-Company, whom I also secretly wanted to be . . . *The Life of Riley* with William Bendix, especially one episode in which he had to count a jar full of jelly beans.

1955: I remember Mary Martin taking the three Darling children on a magical journey to Never-Never Land . . . *Gunsmoke*'s Chester Goode who could have used a good pair of corrective boots . . . Rooting for everyone on *The $64,000 Question,* especially that shoemaker from the Bronx . . . *The Mickey Mouse Club,* even though I was too old for it (Annette, on the other hand, was just right) . . . Sergeant Ernie Bilko and his

conniving cohorts . . . Captain Kangaroo and the impressions of him I used to do in my playroom . . . Perry Como and that song I remember to this day: "Letters/We get letters/We get stacks and stacks of letters/Dear, Perry/Would you be so kind/To fill a request/And sing the song I like best?"

1956: I remember Elvis Presley (from the waist up) on Ed Sullivan's Sunday night show. . . . Chet Huntley and David Brinkley, teamed for the first time to cover the political conventions . . . The wonderful *Wizard of Oz*, shown on the tube for the first time, and for free . . . *Playhouse 90*, and especially its second show, Rod Serling's

Requiem for a Heavyweight . . . Jane Wyman and her anthology series . . . The pure *Price Is Right*, not the gaudy version of the 1970s . . . Bad grammar in "Winston tastes good like a cigarette should" . . . Tennessee Ernie Ford with his own show, after scoring so big on *I Love Lucy*.

1957: I remember Dick Clark and his *American Bandstand* show, originating from Philadelphia. I used to watch the show just to see whether Justine Corelli was wearing a tight sweater or not. . . . Nikita Khrushchev's visit to our shores and his outrage over not being allowed to tour Disneyland . . . *The Tonight Show* was taken over by an ex-game show host, Jack Paar. . . . Erle Stanley Gardner's book character, Perry Mason, came to the tube. . . . Richard Rodgers' original score for a musical version of *Cinderella*, with Julie Andrews as the put-upon stepsister . . . Eddie Haskell on *Leave It to Beaver*.

1958: I remember the quiz show scandals. I lost a little faith in mankind. How could Charles Van Doren, with those honest eyes, be dishonest? . . . that wonderful music for *Peter Gunn* by Henry Mancini (Lola Albright wasn't too shabby either) . . . Fred Astaire traded in Ginger Rogers for a newer model, Barrie Chase, and won a windfall of Emmys. . . . "Kookie, Kookie, lend me your comb," became a familiar phrase on, and off, *77 Sunset Strip*. . . . Ex-baseball player Chuck Connors became a gun-toting cowboy with a young son on *Rifleman*. . . . *Naked City* conjured up visions of an

eight-million-member nudist colony on Staten Island.

1959: I remember the Ponderosa and its residents. . . . Walter Winchell and his staccato narrative for *The Untouchables,* one of my favorite shows . . . a Sunday night staple called *Dennis the Menace* with Jay North whom I met several years later . . . and, earlier that same day, *GE College Bowl* with Allen Ludden asking the questions, most of them beyond me . . . Rod Serling's *Twilight Zone* kept me on the edge of my seat. . . . *Dobie Gillis* began, but I didn't like it, and I can't remember why.

1960: I remember Andy Griffith and Opie and Aunt Bee, but especially Barney Fife, of Mayberry. . . . the great Presidential debates between Richard M. Nixon and John F. Kennedy; Kennedy's cool, calm appearance impressed many, but not my father who voted for Nixon anyway. . . . That freckled chunk of wood named Howdy Doody bowed out of TV and I'll never forget Clarabell uttering his first, and last, words: "Goodbye, kids". . . . the last escapades of Lucy, Ricky, Fred, and Ethel aired in April.

1961: I remember Alan Shepard's fifteen-minute flight into outer space. I watched it in school on TV. . . . Ben Casey and Dr. Kildare and their on-screen surgery; I liked Kildare better. . . . *The Dick Van Dyke Show* bowed and made a star of twenty-three-year-old Mary Tyler Moore. . . . I loved *Hazel,* but not *Mister Ed.* . . . Fred Gwynne and Joe E. Ross made me

laugh as Officers Francis Muldoon and Gunther Toody. . . . Dave Garroway left the *Today* program. . . . Katie Winters had trouble with her deodorant. . . . *Sing Along with Mitch* was so corny that I couldn't bear to watch, or sing.

1962: I remember *The Beverly Hillbillies,* who showed us that down home common sense could outwit big city slickers. . . . Jackie Kennedy's televised tour of the White House . . . Johnny Carson left the game-show circuit to become host of *The Tonight Show.* Groucho Marx was his first guest. . . . We were urged to let Hertz put us in the driver's seat. . . . Julie Andrews joined Carol Burnett for a concert at Carnegie Hall and it was wonderful. . . . A ninety-minute western, *The Virginian,* began.

1963: I remember President Kennedy's funeral, but more vividly the horror of seeing live Lee Harvey Oswald shot. . . . Jerry Lewis's terrible two-hour television

show; thank God (can you say that on TV?) they cancelled it fast. . . . *Petticoat Junction*, on the heels of the *Hillbillies*, began and was another hit for CBS. . . . A one-armed man was pursued by *The Fugitive*, played perfectly by stoic David Janssen. . . . *Mr. Novak* was one of my favorite programs. . . . Hugh Downs began his long stint on the *Today* show. . . . Judy Garland's variety show was long-awaited—especially the week she played hostess to Barbra Streisand and Ethel Merman.

1964: I remember the spate of fantasy shows, some of which I liked, some of which I didn't—*The Munsters, The Addams Family, Bewitched,* and *My Living Doll*. . . . February 16, 1964, when the Beatles made their *Ed Sullivan Show* appearance. They sang "She Loves You" and we sat spellbound. . . . *Gilligan's Island* was so insipid, it was funny. . . . *Flipper* was a Saturday night favorite (I still can hum the theme song).

. . . Jim Nabors left Andy Griffith's show but continued the Gomer Pyle role in his own series. . . . *That Was the Week That Was* was great, especially Nancy Ames singing the opening song, a piece of satirical perfection. . . . *Hullabaloo* and *Shindig* showcased our favorite rock stars and groups.

1965: I remember Bill Cosby and Robert Culp, with their seemingly ad-libbed dialogue on *I Spy*. . . . The National Driver's Test (which I flunked) was one of the first of its kind. . . . An abomination titled *My Mother, the Car* became the butt of numerous jokes about the state of television. . . . Don Adams began a five-year run in *Get Smart!* and I became one of the show's biggest boosters. . . . The Sunday night show that dared to compete with Ed Sullivan did well: *The F.B.I.* (so there *was* an Efrem Zimbalist, Sr.).

1966: I remember Leonard Nimoy's Vulcanized ears (I've heard of a Darwin's point, but this) on *Star Trek*. . . . Batman and Robin were a huge rage twice-a-week. For the kids, it was pure fun; for the adults, one tongue-in-cheek pun after another. . . . A scary afternoon soap opera on ABC called *Dark Shadows* had a vampire as a regular character (he didn't moonlight as a hematologist). . . . Television cashed in on the Beatles and created *The Monkees* starring one of my boyhood favorites, Micky Dolenz of *Circus Boy*. . . . Tammy Grimes' ill-fated sitcom didn't even last through September.

1967: I remember a fall special I loved so much that I hoped it would become a regular series—*Laugh-In*. . . . Raymond Burr came back to TV after a long run as Perry Mason, managing to capture lightning twice, as Ironside. . . . *He and She* was a sophisticated comedy, but apparently there were not enough sophisticated Americans to watch, and it was cancelled after winning an Emmy. . . . *Captain Nice* and *Mr. Terrific*, both super hero spoofs, debuted the same day on different networks. They both died in seventeen weeks. . . . Carol Burnett began her fabulously successful variety show (she once admitted it wouldn't last thirteen weeks).

1968: I remember the violence of the Chicago political convention. The cameras caught it all. . . . Diahann Carroll, sans singing, came to television as a funny nurse. . . . CBS's *Sixty Minutes* probed matters with aplomb. . . . I never liked Jack Lord until *Hawaii Five-O* began its run, and I'm still watching. . . . *The Mod Squad* was perfect for the 1960s, but it never was something I stayed home to watch. . . . Hope Lange was wonderful as Mrs. Caroline Muir. . . . My friend Phyllis Diller tried again, this time with a variety show, and flopped again. . . . Truman Capote wrote a beautiful play called *The Thanksgiving Visitor* which renewed my faith in television.

1969: I remember Tiny Tim and Miss Vicky getting hitched on *The Tonight Show* (did *Today* carry the divorce??). . . . The Smothers Brothers were embroiled in political controversy on their CBS show and the network cancelled them. . . . On July 20th, Neil Armstrong walked on the moon and we were there. . . . Michael Parks did a motorcycle version of *Route 66* which was just okay. . . . A new face, Dick Cavett, entered the talk show field. He became the most literate, but lowest-rated, of the bunch. . . . Big Bird, Kermit the Frog, and Bob McGrath enthralled young kids, including my New Jersey nieces, on *Sesame Street.*

1970: I remember Geraldine Jones, Flip Wilson's female impersonation. . . . Mary Tyler Moore made an enormous career comeback on her own sitcom, after a series of flop movies and a disastrous Broadway play. . . . *The Partridge Family* brought to life the real rock group, The Cowsills, and David Cassidy, age 20, became an idol of millions. . . . Burt Reynolds played a detective by the name of Dan August. . . . Neil Simon's play, *The Odd Couple,* was a huge TV hit, but his other effort, *Barefoot in the Park,* died fast. . . . *Marcus Welby* starred Robert Young of *Father Knows Best* fame, and it was a huge success.

1971: I remember *All in the Family*'s premiere. I sat there shocked at the language and amused by the best jokes ever. I loved it immediately. . . . I was happy there were no more cigarette commercials. . . . I thought *Columbo* was one of the best show in years. . . . I felt sorry for Dick Van Dyke being trapped in a sitcom turkey. . . . I couldn't see a show like *Longstreet.* . . . Hugh Downs retired from

149

the *Today* show. . . . Ed Sullivan was retired by CBS after a long and distinguished career. . . . Merv Griffin gave up his network late-night talk show to return to a syndicated version.

1972: I remember Karl Malden and Kirk Douglas's son, Michael, in *The Streets of San Francisco.* . . . *The Waltons,* with one of my favorite actors Richard Thomas and my neighbor, Will Geer . . . President Nixon traveled to China and Russia and was reelected—TV covered it all (can't blame television). . . . *Maude* was spun-off *All in the Family* making Lear the King of Comedy. . . . *Kung Fu* was a popular show, but a half-hour after watching it. . . . *The Rookies* showed us another side of police work, life with *young* incompetents. . . . *Bridget Loves Bernie* was a charming show, created by playwright *(Same Time, Next Year)* Bernard Slade, but it got shot down by Jewish and Catholic pressure groups, who had apparently never heard of *Abie's Irish Rose.*

1973: I remember the William Loud family of Santa Barbara, California, subjects of the PBS documentary, *An American Family* (Lance is now a member of a punk rock band called The Mumps). . . . Bill Bixby starred in his third series, *The Magician,* but the show lacked (you guessed it) magic. . . . Norman Lear brought X-rated nightclub comic Redd Foxx to TV as Fred Sanford doing an updated version of *Amos 'n' Andy.* . . . I loved Dom DeLuise's sitcom, *Lotsa Luck!,* every bit as good as the old *Honeymooners* show. . . . Movie star William

Holden showed up several times in a dramatization of the Wambaugh book, *The Blue Knight.*

1974: I remember Sonny Bono falling on his face—everyone but ABC knew he would. . . . Alan Alda was the perfect choice to bring *M*A*S*H* to the little screen. . . . *Upstairs, Downstairs* proved once again that the British were not only coming, they were here to stay. . . . Valerie Harper got her own show, *Rhoda.* . . . *Born Free* suffered a still birth and was soon cancelled. . . . CBS put a lot of money into *Planet of the Apes,* but they couldn't capture the charm of the movie. . . . Freddie Prinze, the brilliant young comedian from New York, became an overnight success in *Chico & the Man,* and then, less than three years later, took his own life.

1975: I remember the emergence of *Happy Days* and how quickly Henry Winkler's character, "the Fonz," caught on. . . . *The Sound of Music* came to TV and racked up some big numbers. . . . Howard Cosell made a fool of himself as he tried to play Ed Sullivan and failed (a tall order). . . . David Soul from the old *Here Come the Brides* show and Paul Michael Glaser were Starsky and Hutch, or were they Hutch and Starsky. Who cares . . . it bored me anyway. . . . CBS hoped to capture the essence of *Upstairs, Downstairs* in their ambitious production, *Beacon Hill,* but it was a dismal failure (I fell asleep halfway through the first show).

1976: I remember *Gone With the Wind,* with 148 commercials. . . . *Alice* was not quite the same as its movie counterpart, but it was fun and the kid was charming. . . . *Mary Hartman, Mary Hartman* worried about the waxy buildup on linoleum but not about mass murders in Fernwood, Ohio. . . . Nancy Walker, who quit *Rhoda* and *McMillan and Wife,* toplined two series. Defeated, she went back to *Rhoda.* . . . Kate Jackson, Farrah Fawcett-Majors, and Jaclyn Smith were the biggest things in TV.

1977: I remember Bob Newhart and Carol Burnett who both decided to call it quits. . . . *Eight Is Enough,* the modern version of *The Waltons.* . . . A prime time soap opera spoof, *Soap,* that caused nationwide concern over the morals of our youth. . . . Donny and Marie Osmond moved to Utah to do their variety show so they'd be closer to the Mormon Church (to pray for better ratings?). . . . Gavin McLeod, who left a hot series, made it big again on *The Love Boat,* sort of a *Love, American Style* on the high seas. . . . ABC managed to become the number one network for the first time in its long history.

Housebreaking Lassie

"Daddy, tell me a story," pleaded the little daughter of author Eric Knight back in 1938 on a farm in Bucks County, Pennsylvania. It had been a chronic cry of the little girl whose father was a best-selling storyteller of such works as *The Flying Yorkshireman.*

Knight concocted a sentimental tale about a faithful collie dog, separated from her poor but honest young master, who makes a tortuous, 200-mile journey from Scotland back to England and the arms of her family. At the urging of his wife, Knight wrote and peddled the story to the old *Saturday Evening Post.* It was such a hit that a publisher, Winston, persuaded him to expand it into a full-length book. Knight did, and it was published in 1940 under the title *Lassie Come Home.*

Seeing its possibilities as a film, MGM producer Sam Marx contacted Knight and bought the right to *Lassie* for the meager some of $8,000, that included all theatrical rights in perpetuity. Neither Knight nor his heirs ever saw another penny from *Lassie.*

By 1942, Marx had developed a script from Knight's book, but was having a real problem: he couldn't find a dog. It was a well known fact that pure-bred collies are impossibly high-strung animals. An urgent call was sent out to every major trainer, kennel and dog show in the country. Desperate, Marx once "auditioned" 300 yapping pooches in the old Hollywood Stars baseball park, all to no avail.

Among the rejected rovers was "Pal," owned by a trainer named Rudd Weatherwax. The runt of an unpedigreed litter, Pal had the unpleasant habit of

The original Lassie *company. (L-r) Tommy Rettig, Lassie, George Cleveland, Donald Keeler, his dog Pokey, Jan Clayton.*

chasing cars. Weatherwax, who ran a kennel, had in fact acquired the dog in payment of a $10 kennel (he ran a kennel) debt. Not knowing what to do with the animal, Rudd turned him out on a friend's ranch to run wild.

There he might have remained forever if it had not been for two things. One was a violent rainstorm in the San Joaquin Valley, and the other was the persistence of Weatherwax. Knowing full well the difficulties of training pure-bred collies, he kept boring in on and being rejected by the MGM Marx. Just then, the San Joaquin River overflowed its banks. Marx got a hurry call from the production office: if he could get a dog and a second unit contingent upstate within 24 hours, he would have the most exciting adventure material ever seen in a B-picture (which *Lassie Come Home* started out as). Marx pictured the whole thing in his movie-minded mind: courageous collie, half dead with weariness, fights the raging torrent in order to be reunited with Roddy McDowall. All wet dogs looked alike, Marx reasoned. Later he could find the right one. Right now, though, he had to move fast. He hired Pal.

Pal performed like a trooper. The director, Fred Wilcox, puts it this way:

The angelic-faced Jon Provost was only seven years old when tapped for his Lassie role and already a veteran of ten films.

(L-r) Jon Sheppod, Jon Provost, Cloris Leachman, Lassie. Lassie's second format, 1957 to 1958.

A September 1957 Lassie *episode featured a young orphan, Timmy who showed up at the Miller farm, and stayed until 1964.*

"That dog dove into the river as Pal but he came out Lassie."

The film was a smash, out-box-officed *Mrs. Miniver* at New York's Radio City Music Hall, and plans were set immediately to film a sequel and another and another and another. Lassie was being touted as "Greer Garson with fur" and MGM placed her on its star roster between Hedy Lamarr and Myrna Loy. Six sequels followed, each one turning a tidy profit. But by 1950, inexpensive series pictures were a drag on the market due to the inroads made by the new medium, television. So, in 1952, the studio gave Weatherwax rights to the property in lieu of the $40,000 it still owed the trainer on his contract, a decision MGM is ruing to this day.

Weatherwax turned *Lassie* over to a shrewd producer named Robert Maxwell (in return for ten percent of the profits) who made a deal with CBS for a television series based on the *Lassie* films, but with continuing characters. Maxwell began shooting the first of the *Lassie* TV shows in 1953, and on September 12, 1954, the program premiered.

TV Guide's listing for that show: "The famous Hollywood canine will be featured in a series of dramatic stories starring Tommy Rettig as her master. In the first film, young Jeff Miller inherits Lassie from a relative but is puzzled by his new pet's strange behavior. Lassie keeps returning to her former home until Jeff finally learns the dead master's secret."

Tommy Rettig, then nearly thirteen, played Lassie's little master for three seasons (103 episodes). Starring with him were former musical star Jan Clayton as his widowed mother Ellen, and character actor George Cleveland as Gramps. However, Lassie was clearly the star. She alone received 2,000 fan letters every week, compared to the 3,000 received by the rest of the cast. Her salary was $1,500 per show, but she earned $2,000 for a personal appearance (county fairs, supermarket openings, etc.), making her one of the few animals who grossed over $100,000 a year.

But in October, 1956, Maxwell decided to sell *Lassie,* thereby making the same mistake his predecessors had: He underestimated the animal's staying powers. However, at the time, it seemed a good idea. The bland Middlewestern farm format, the boy, the dog and the lovable grandpa looking out for the widowed mother, was wearing thin. And Rettig, right smack in the middle of puberty, was beginning to look too mature for the role. How long could a good thing last, he reasoned.

So when an oil-rich young Texan named Jack Wrather came into the scene and offered $3,250,000, Maxwell jumped. The latter was retained as *Lassie*'s producer.

Problems with the cast, aside from Rettig's spurt in growth, began. Rettig's mother, an ambitious woman who was quick to realize that her son was pivotal, needed to be appeased constantly. Ultimately, this caught up with Jan Clayton whose personal fondness for Tommy fanned her resentment of Mrs. Rettig's attitude. Weatherwax had his problems, too. The original Pal, by the time the TV show came around, was too old. So Rudd pressed into service Pal's son, Pal II, the original TV Lassie. (In 1957, Pal III took over the role, and, in 1961, figured in a divorce suit brought by Mrs. Weatherwax, who asked for a "division" of the dog, whose value she placed at $100,000.)

The first big crisis occurred, predictably, in early 1957. Tommy was too old, Jan Clayton felt she was in a creative rut and the wholesome farm wardrobe was beginning to bug her, and Cleveland turned sick and eventually died in July 1957.

Maxwell and Wrather held a summit meeting. How to ease out the old and bring in the new without shaking up *Lassie's* hardcore following (some 33 million viewers) too much. It was as delicate as a surgical operation. Wrather had spotted seven-year-old Jon Provost in a movie, *Escapade in Japan,* the boy's tenth film. He was a wistful child, small for his age (a requisite). Maxwell, who wrote the transition script ("The Runaway," which aired in September, 1957), decided to make him into an orphan who arrives unexpectedly at the Miller farm. He would be welcomed by Tommy Rettig and Miss Clayton, who then, after a decent interval

(less than 13 weeks), would be shipped off to the big city. Lassie would be inherited by young Provost as the new boy, Timmy, who in turn would inherit a new set of parents through adoption.

Cloris Leachman and Jon Sheppod became the parents, and a fine character actor, George Chandler, was added as Uncle Petrie to, more or less, replace the deceased Cleveland. The year of Leachman and Sheppod and Chandler was one of the stormiest in show business history, a year

George Chandler portrayed Uncle Petrie, a relative of the Martins. He was dropped from the cast when viewers urged the show to "warm up" the relationship between Timmy and his father.

of sharp personality conflicts and falling ratings. Miss Leachman, who, of course, went on to TV stardom as Phyllis Lindstrom on *The Mary Tyler Moore Show* and her own show, was a New York actress who was temperamentally unsuited to her *Lassie* assignment, which she described as "playing house." She immediately fell into conflict with Chandler, and the two of them fought bitterly for the entire season she was there. She just couldn't understand why the dog got all the close-ups. Sheppod, new to the business, was too unsure of himself to help matters any. And Chandler suffered by comparison to Cleveland.

The *Lassie* farm became a cold and somehow forbidding place. Viewers noticed, too, and sent letters of protest to the network, saying that Leachman and Sheppod were "too stiff." Wrather took over (Maxwell had departed by this time), dumped the two parents, "deemphasized" Chandler (later he was dropped altogether), and imported a new parental team, June Lockhart and Hugh Reilly.

It worked magically. For almost seven solid seasons Provost played Timmy Martin in 156 *Lassie* shows. Lockhart and Reilly were taken to the bosoms of America until, alas, September 6, 1964.

The show, the first of the new season, began like any other *Lassie* episode. A prerecorded whistler trilled the theme song, a juvenile voice hollered "L-a-s-s-i-e!" and 35 million viewers settled back for another half-hour with the peripatetic collie. When it ended, loyal *Lassie*-ites were shocked. June Lockhart, Hugh Reilly, and Jon Provost has wrung out final farewells to Lassie,

A fugitive from the New York stage, Jan Clayton appeared in the original company of Carousel.

punctuated by crescendos of weepy violins. Yes, dog-eared (sorry) *Lassie* was getting a new look.

This change had been in the planning stages since March, 1963, when the Wrather Corporation suddenly realized that Jon Provost, like his predecessor Tommy Rettig, had become too old for the part, thirteen. The company also discovered that the shows were getting redundant. They lacked freshness. People were beginning to tire of that old farmhouse near Calverton. So in December the cast was forced, by contract, of course, to participate in a bizarre ceremony: its own execution. Two possible endings were shot; Wrather called them "two separations."

The one that aired was a five-part *Lassie* saga, filmed on location in the Sierras. It was a story of survival, much like the original *Lassie Come Home* story thought up in the late 1930s. The Martins journeyed to Lake Superior for vacation where Lassie, Timmy, and the father embarked upon a fishing trip. A quick squall materialized, the fishing boat overturned, and Lassie was separated from Provost and Reilly. The dog was miraculously saved by a forest ranger and nursed back to health for four succeeding half-hours. At the conclusion of the five parts, Timmy and his parents conveniently reappeared, reclaimed the dog and returned to the farm. This series of episodes was a definite attempt to introduce a character and see how he would be accepted by the public.

The first of the epic quintet was aired in early February, 1964. This and the four other adventures made big news. *Lassie* was back in the Top Ten, an almost unheard of situation for a show on the air that long (ten years).

Robert Bray, the actor who played the forest ranger, Corey Stuart, was an immediate hit. Fan mail poured in, and it was evident to the Wrather folk that the Martin family needed to be "killed off." It was important to the storyline that the Martins would have to go some place where they couldn't take Lassie with them.

At first, the producers favored the idea of having Paul, the father, join the Peace Corps, until Sargent Shriver's office in Washington revealed that the Peace Corp didn't forbid dogs. The solution, after many hours of research, turned out to be Australia. The Martins would be dumped into the Australian bush as homesteaders, giving up the lush life in America to till poor farmland overseas.

As the final farewell script was written, the family began packing for the long trip when they discovered they could not take

Lassie with Robert Bray who played forest ranger Corey Stuart.

Lassie along. The dog would need to be quarantined in England for six months before being allowed entry into Australia. Naturally, it would have broken Lassie's heart to be penned up for a half a year, so the Martins left her with a neighbor, Cully, played by Andy Clyde. This was the first of three transitional episodes. Two weeks later, Bray, as Ranger Stuart, was reintroduced in a touching scene with Lassie. Cully was stricken with a heart attack and Lassie summons Stuart to help the old codger. Unable to care for the dog, Cully gives her to Stuart, rounding out the final sequence, and giving *Lassie* a new look, and a new star.

Bray was one of half a dozen actors tested for the part. Finally the field was narrowed down to two men—Bray and a well-known Western player. The producer, the sponsor, and the ad agency people all preferred the "name" actor. But Lassie liked Bray, and so did millions of viewers, who soon forgot all about the family far away in Australia.

Bray played the role through the 1971 TV season, when *Lassie* was cancelled by CBS and went into syndication.

If someone had told the late Eric Knight what was going to result from his innocent tale. . . .

FUNNYGRAMS

The situation comedy has been television's most durable and successful form. Literally hundreds of sitcoms have aired over the years, as many as thirty-eight during one season (1964–65). Can you identify these comedies by their cryptic descriptions?

1. Betty Jo enters the annual Shady Rest Horseshoe Tournament.

2. Pete Ball mistakes some Vichyssoise for a pot of wallpaper paste.

3. Norman gives the Corbetts a special gift.

4. The entire family pitches in to help Dagmar prepare for her first military ball.

5. Incensed when Mel hires a waiter for more money than they're earning, Flo and Vera turn in their uniforms.

6. Robinson and Nancy stop off at his mother's house for a rest before they return to summer school.

7. The Finches have agreed on the exchange program and now all Eddie Walker has to do is tell his wife.

8. Gabe persuades Vinnie to run for the office of student body president.

9. Bentley decides to send Kelly to a girls' finishing school so that she will acquire some polish.

10. Rusty has accidentally broken his dad's golf clubs, and thinks maybe things won't get so bad if he can talk Linda into taking the blame.

11. Paula and Dick try to aid and comfort their fireman friend Harry.

12. Barbara, who feels she is always in the background because of her famous sister Margaret, decides to become a professional singer.

13. Dr. Wilson invites his neighbor, Donald Peterson, on a fishing trip and learns an important lesson in psychology.

14. Toody and Muldoon head the entertainment committee for the Christmas party at the precinct.

15. Florida is on the rampage, and her bewildered family is at a loss to explain her irritability.

OUT OF THIS WORLD

Science fiction and fantasy are two fields currently riding the crest of popularity in books and films. But television has long considered this genre a fertile field. Here are some extraterrestrial queries for "spaced out" TV fans.

1. What TV program began with the narration, "There is nothing wrong with your television set, do not attempt to adjust the picture. We are controlling the transmission . . ."?

2. Who was the "Sky Marshal of the Universe"?

3. Name the architect who witnessed the invasion of outer space aliens on *The Invaders.*

4. What governmental body put Steve Austin back together again?

5. Where did Samantha and Darrin Stephens reside?

6. What was special about the characters Daniel Weston and Peter Brady?

7. Who played Mrs. John Burton, a girl with something extra?

8. Who was the evil robot on *Captain Video and His Video Rangers*?

9. What was located in an underground complex known as the Tic Toc Base?

10. How did George and Marian Kerby and their dog Neil become ghosts?

11. Who was a Chicago reporter for the Independent News Service and sought out the bizarre and the supernatural?

12. In what form was Abigail Crabtree reincarnated?

13. Name the family who became lost in space.

14. How did Tony Nelson discover Jeannie?

15. Who was the host of *Night Gallery*?

BASED ON THE MOVIE

Television has borrowed ideas from a variety sources: radio, the comics, books, real life, and, of course, the fertile field of movies. Here's a quiz designed to determine how well you recall series based on movies. Fill in the corresponding missing person in each foursome, and name the movie/TV series in which both pairs appeared.

1. William Powell is to————, as Peter Lawford is to Phyllis Kirk.

2. Rex Harrison is to Gene Tierney, as Edward Mulhare is to ————.

3. Lionel Barrymore is to Lew Ayres, as ———— is to Richard Chamberlain.

4. ———— is to Walter Matthau, as Tony Randall is to Jack Klugman.

5. Loretta Young is to ————, as Inger Stevens is to William Windom.

6. Spencer Tracy is to Katharine Hepburn, as Ken Howard is to ————.

7. Glenn Ford is to ————, as Bill Bixby is to Brandon Cruz.

8. Ann Revere is to Elizabeth Taylor, as ———— is to Lori Martin.

9. Constance Bennett is to Cary Grant, as Anne Jeffreys is to ————.

10. ———— is to Doris Day, as Mark Miller is to Patricia Crowley.

11. Preston Foster is to Roddy McDowall, as Gene Evans is to ————.

12. Irene Dunne is to ————, as Peggy Wood is to Rosemary Rice.

13. Yul Brynner is to Deborah Kerr, as ———— is to Samantha Eggar.

14. Spencer Tracy is to Joan Bennett, as ——— is to Ruth Warrick.

15. Arthur Lake is to Penny Singleton, as Will Hutchins is to ————.

16. Tatum O'Neal is to Ryan O'Neal, as Jodie Foster is to ————.

17. Elliott Gould is to Donald Sutherland, as ———— is to Alan Alda.

18. Johnny Sheffield is to Johnny Weissmuller, as ———— is to Ron Ely.

19. Lee Aaker is to John Wayne, as Buddy Foster is to ————.

20. Alan Ladd is to Brandon de Wilde, as ———— is to Chris Shea.

PHOTO SESSION

"Good evening Mr. and Mrs. North America and all the ships at sea" was Walter Winchell's broadcasting trademark. Winchell hosted a news commentary show in 1952, starred in an unsuccessful variety series in 1960, but is probably best remembered as the narrator of The Untouchables.

Ed McConnell hosted Smilin' Ed's Gang, a children's variety show which began in 1950. After McConnell's death in 1955, popular film character actor Andy Devine took over the hosting helm.

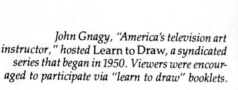

John Gnagy, "America's television art instructor," hosted Learn to Draw, a syndicated series that began in 1950. Viewers were encouraged to participate via "learn to draw" booklets.

Bob Barker must be TV's most durable performer. At least that's what Guinness says: since his debut on Truth or Consequences in 1956, Barker has appeared in 3,524 installments of the game show.

Behind-the-scenes at Flipper, the Ivan Tors adventure series for NBC. Here a sequence is being filmed to look as though actor Brian Kelly is swimming toward the porthole of a sunken sub.

Commando Cody, *played by Judd Holdren, was a popular 1955 NBC children's series. The "Sky Marshall of the Universe" was assisted by Joan Albright who was played by Aline Towne.*

Carol Burnett was known to TV audiences as Garry Moore's femme foil. In 1967, CBS granted her a variety show and teamed her with Harvey Korman and young Vicky Lawrence (of the Young Americans singing ensemble). The show lasted eleven years and is now a success in syndication.

Featured here in a 1955 Kraft Television Theatre production of F. Scott Fitzgerald's The Diamond As Big as the Ritz, young Elizabeth Montgomery went on to TV fame as Samantha Stephens, the witch in Bewitched, a 1964 Screen Gems entry.

You Bet Your Life was more of a showcase for Groucho's wit and wisdom than a serious quiz show. One of TV's most popular pairings was George Fenneman, as announcer, and Groucho Marx, as quizmaster, together for eleven profitable years.

The Thin Man *was MGM's very* first *effort into TV production. Peter Lawford and Phyllis Kirk played Nick and Nora Charles, roles created in the movies by William Powell and Myrna Loy. Here they pose with their pet terrier, Asta.*

Comedian Bob Newhart was a popular entertainer on the nightclub circuit when he came to TV in 1961. Although his show did not strike gold, it did win an Emmy, a sign of his ingenuity. Ten years later, Newhart returned to the tube in a sitcom which ran six years.

Alfred Hitchcock was a welcome addition to TV when he brought his bizarre wit, via Alfred Hitchcock Presents, to television in 1955. Though he didn't direct every episode of the TV show, he did read each script and, of course, introduced all the episodes with his mandatory, "Good evening."

Jinx Falkenberg was a favorite pin-up girl and movie starlet in the forties. She joined Bob Hope and Irving Berlin for a Christmas tour of Germany in 1947, but came to TV in the early fifties when she and her husband, Tex McCrary, interviewed literally thousands of celebrities on their show, Tex and Jinx.

Donald May played Cadet Charles C. Thompson on West Point, an anthology series featuring dramatizations of life at the famous military school. The show ran only one year on ABC in 1957, but May later showed up in other TV programs.

Frank Gallop, announcer for Perry Como, "hosted" Light's Out, a 30-minute live melodrama on NBC.

"Queen of the Super Circus" was beautiful Mary Hartline. Here she poses with a doll bearing her name, one of the countless pieces of merchandise that cashed in on the popularity of stars in the fifties TV scene.

Former Miss America, Lee Meriwether, clowns with J. Fred Muggs, both of the Today *show. Muggs looks friendly here, but he bit Dave Garroway more than once.*

Kay Kyser played the Professor of The College of Musical Knowledge, *a quiz musical show which debuted in 1949 on NBC. Kyser retired in 1954 and was replaced by newcomer Tennessee Ernie Ford.*

Winky Dink and You *was a children's show with audience participation stressed. Over two million Winky Dink Magic Kits were sold in a short time. Consisting of a transparent plastic sheet which was placed over the TV screen, and crayons, children could assist their cartooned hero, Winky Dink, by drawing in the proper object on the screen. Jack Barry, the show's creator, hosted the CBS series from 1953—1957. Here he is shown with young Harlan Barnard.*

The singing McGuire sisters were three of Arthur Godfrey's best "friends" during the fifties.

Dean Martin and Jerry Lewis appeared on The Colgate Comedy Hour on a rotating basis for over six seasons. They were on the very top of the money-making TV performers when they split in 1956 to pursue their separate careers.

Renzo Cesana was The Continental to many female viewers who watched his 1952 CBS series. They loved his sophistication.

Gertrude Berg not only starred in the classic series, The Goldbergs, but also is credited with creating and writing the show which began as a radio show. Here she is shown chatting with her agent, Ted Ashley.

Colonel Terry Lee (played by John Baer, front row, left) inherited an Oriental gold mine from his deceased grandfather. His search for it and battle against evil made up the thirty-minute DuMont network children's show, based on the comic strip, Terry and the Pirates (1952).

Buckskin was a 1958 summer entry for NBC. Young Tommy Nolan portrayed the fatherless, harmonica-playing Jody O'Connell of Buckskin, Montana, during the 1880's. Sallie Brophie played his mother, Annie, owner of the town's hotel.

ANSWERS

AULD ACQUAINTANCES *(page 2)*

1. c	8. a	15. s
2. b	9. q	16. g
3. l	10. d	17. n
4. k	11. r	18. i
5. p	12. o	19. h
6. m	13. f	20. t
7. j	14. e	

HUSBANDS *(page 4)*

1. Jane
2. Vinnie
3. Peg
4. Laura
5. Ethel
6. Nora
7. Emily
8. Margaret
9. Trixie
10. Georgette
11. Dorothy
12. Blanche
13. Maureen
14. Alice
15. Jerry

WIVES *(page 5)*

1. Jim
2. Jim
3. Jim
4. Herb
5. Mike
6. Cosmo
7. James
8. George
9. George
10. Luke
11. Stewart
12. Martin
13. Don
14. Alex
15. Jake

TV CONNECTIONS *(page 6)*

1. Herbert Anderson co-starred with Jay North in *Dennis the Menace,* and Sajid Khan shared star billing with North on *Maya.*
2. Patricia Harty played comic strip character Blondie in the 1968 TV series while Pamela Britton played Mrs. Bumstead in the 1954 TV show.
3. Doris Day and Judy Carne both resided in San Francisco in their respective sitcoms, *The Doris Day Show* and *Love On a Rooftop.*
4. Paul Lynde starred in *The New Temperature's Rising* and James Whitmore starred in *Temperature's Rising.*
5. Wally Cox played a teacher at Jefferson Junior High in *Mr. Peepers* while James Franciscus played a teacher at Jefferson High School in *Mr. Novak.*
6. Both Richard Widmark and Harpo Marx appeared as themselves on 1955 episodes of *I Love Lucy.*
7. Both Roger C. Carmel and Richard Deacon played Roger Buell, husband to Kaye Ballard, on *The Mothers-in-Law.*
8. Ken Curtis played Festus Hagen and Dennis Weaver portrayed Chester Goode, deputies to Marshal Matt Dillon on *Gunsmoke.*
9. Both Ms. Rountree and Mr. Spivak were hosts of *Meet the Press.*
10. Raymond Massey starred in the 1956 syndicated series *I Spy,* an anthology, while Bill Cosby co-starred in *I Spy,* a 1965 adventure series on NBC.
11. Stanley Fafara played Whitey and Stephen Talbot portrayed Gilbert, friends of Beaver Cleaver on *Leave It to Beaver.*
12. Steve Allen and Garry Moore were both hosts of *I've Got a Secret.*
13. Smiley Burnette played Charley Pratt and Rufe Davis played Floyd Smoot, engineers on the *Cannonball,* the train serving *Petticoat Junction.*
14. Pat Priest and Beverley Owen both played Marilyn Munster, the niece, on *The Munsters.*
15. Vincent Price portrayed Egghead, and Otto Preminger played Mr. Freeze, arch villians of Batman.
16. The voice of Betty Rubble on *The Flinstones* was provided by both Ms. Benaderet and Mrs. Hartwig.
17. Don Knotts co-starred with Andy Griffith on *The Andy Griffith Show,* and Jerry Van Dyke co-starred with Griffith on *Headmaster.*
18. Paul Lynde played Paul Simms, a Santa Barbara attorney on *The Paul Lynde Show;* Arthur Hill played Owen Marshall, a Santa Barbara attorney on *Owen Marshall.*
19. Anthony George played Tony Vincente and John Sylvester played Keith Barron, Joanne's (Mary Stuart) husbands on *Search for Tomorrow.*
20. Lee Bowman and Hugh Marlowe both played sleuth Ellery Queen on various versions of the program.

UP, UP AND AWAY *(page 14)*

1. The Standish Arms
2. Perry White, *Daily Planet* editor
3. Smallville, U.S.A.
4. Krypton
5. Kellogg's cereals
6. Jack Larson
7. Miss Lane
8. Kal-El
9. *I Love Lucy*
10. Los Angeles City Hall
11. Eben and Martha Kent
12. Great Caesar's
13. Robert Shayne
14. Speeding bullet, locomotive, tall buildings
15. Lois Lane
16. Herburt Vigran
17. In the Store Room
18. Aunt Louisa
19. Professor Pepperwinkle
20. Phyllis Coates and Noel Neill

WHO SAID IT? *(page 18)*

1. Kathryn Murray
2. Jackie Gleason as Ralph Kramden
3. Ricky Nelson
4. William Bendix as Chester A. Riley
5. George Gobel
6. Bob Keeshan as Captain Kangaroo
7. Red Skelton
8. Richard Simmons as Sergeant Preston
9. Peter Potter
10. Louis Nye
11. Liberace
12. Don McNeill
13. Jack Bailey
14. Jay North as Dennis Mitchell
15. Don Adams as Maxwell Smart
16. Steve Allen
17. Desi Arnaz as Ricky Ricardo
18. John Daly
19. Dave Garroway
20. Ruth Gilbert as Maxine

COULD YOU HAVE HIT THE JACKPOT? *(page 21)*

1. Twenty-two (as of 1956)
2. Africa
3. *Lucky Lady II*
4. Eight
5. Auguste Rodin
6. 1863
7. Ted Williams
8. a. Winner had 14
   b. Five
   c. Seventeen
9. *I Was a Communist for the FBI*
10. Callander, Ontario
11. Christopher Columbus
12. Theodore Roosevelt
13. *Twelve O'Clock High*
14. *Mona Lisa*
15. Leon Cadore, Brooklyn and Joe Oeschger, Boston
16. Falstaff
17. a. Winner had 17
    b. Seven
    c. Ten
18. Billy the Kid
19. Tripolitan
20. Napoleon Bonaparte (Rip took a "nap")
21. Gaul
22. Ambrosia
23. *The Time of Your Life*

PRIVATE I'S . . . *(page 32)*

1. Mark Saber
2. Edie Hart
3. Chester Morris
4. Martin Kane
5. Amos Burke
6. Frank Lovejoy
7. Cricket Blake
8. Paul Drake
9. Honey West
10. Frank Smith
11. Francis DeSales
12. Nick Charles
13. Tom Tully
14. Darren McGavin
15. Ellery Queen

THE LUCILLE BALL PUZZLE *(page 30)*

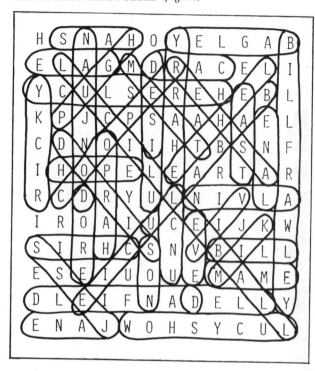

THAT FAMILIAR FACE *(page 43)*

1. GALE GORDON: *The Brothers; Our Miss Brooks; Dennis the Menace; The Lucy Show.*
2. TED BESSELL: *It's a Man's World; Gomer Pyle, U.S.M.C.; Me and the Chimp; That Girl.*
3. RICHARD DEACON: *The Charlie Farrell Show; The Dick Van Dyke Show; Leave It to Beaver; The Mothers-in-Law.*
4. RICHARD CRENNA: *The Real McCoys; Our Miss Brooks; Slattery's People; All's Fair.*
5. MARION LORNE: *Bewitched; Sally; The Garry Moore Show; Mr. Peepers.*
6. BURT REYNOLDS: *Gunsmoke; Hawk; Riverboat; Dan August.*
7. JUDY CARNE: *The Baileys of Balboa; Fair Exchange; Laugh-In; Love on a Rooftop.*
8. DOUG MCCLURE: *Overland Trail; Search; The Virginian; Barbary Coast.*
9. NANCY WALKER: *The Mary Tyler Moore Show; Rhoda; Family Affair; Blansky's Beauties; McMillan and Wife.*
10. DICK VAN DYKE: *Laugh Line; The Dick Van Dyke Show; The New Dick Van Dyke Show; The Carol Burnett Show.*
11. BUDDY EBSEN: *The Beverly Hillbillies; Northwest Passage; Davy Crockett; Barnaby Jones.*
12. RICHARD LONG: *Nanny and the Professor; The Big Valley; Thicker than Water; Bourbon Street Beat.*
13. PAUL LYNDE: *Bewitched; The Paul Lynde Show; The Munsters; The New Temperature's Rising.*
14. NORMAN FELL: *The 87th Precinct; Dan August; Needles and Pins; Three's Company.*
15. DICK VAN PATTEN: *The New Dick Van Dyke Show; Mama; Eight Is Enough; The Partners.*

AND NOW A WORD FROM . . . *(page 44)*

1. e
2. j
3. s
4. r
5. g
6. b
7. l
8. o
9. k
10. a
11. f
12. q
13. p
14. d
15. n
16. m
17. i
18. h
19. t
20. c

THE DIVINE MISS EMMY *(page 60)*

1948: *Pantomime Quiz Time*
1949: *Time for Beany*
1950: Groucho Marx
1951: Sid Caesar
1952: *Dragnet*
1953: *Victory at Sea*
1954: *Disneyland*
1955: Phil Silvers
1956: Perry Como
1957: *The Comedian*
1958: *Maverick*
1959: *Huckleberry Hound*
1960: *Macbeth*
1961: *The Defenders*
1962: Shirley Booth
1963: *The Danny Kaye Show*
1964: *The Dick Van Dyke Show*
1965: *The Fugitive*
1966: *The Monkees*
1967: *Mission: Impossible*
1968: *Laugh-In*
1969: *Room 222*
1970: *The Flip Wilson Show*
1971: *Elizabeth R*
1972: Scott Jacoby
1973: William Holden
1974: Robert Blake
1975: *NBC's Saturday Night*

HOW WELL DO YOU KNOW THE BUNKERS? *(page 52)*

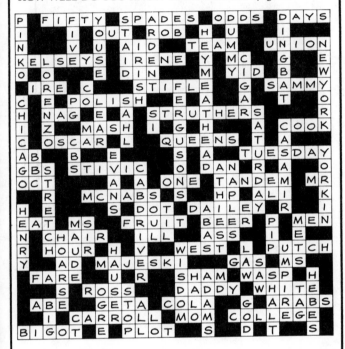

WHO AM I? *(page 64)*

1. Fang, a/k/a K-13
2. Flipper the dolphin, or Pete the pelican
3. King
4. Spot
5. Lassie
6. Bimbo
7. Flicka
8. Buttons
9. Cleo, the bassett hound, on *The People's Choice*
10. Scruffy
11. Demosthenes
12. Asta
13. Judy
14. Ben
15. Tramp
16. Enoch, Charlie, and Cindy
17. Mister Ed
18. Fury
19. Jasper
20. Kit Kat

FRIENDLY PERSUASIONS *(page 67)*

1. Dexter Franklin
2. Beverly
3. Todd Russell
4. Clipper
5. Mrs. McGillicuddy
6. Nancy Remington
7. Mr. Thackery
8. Mrs. Davis
9. Mr. Beasley
10. Jane Stacy
11. Jake Goldberg
12. Oriole
13. Babs
14. Dr. Bombay
15. Freddie Wilson
16. Rosie
17. Jamie
18. Anne
19. Margaret McDonald
20. Mr. Schuyler

CAN YOU PICTURE THIS? *(page 68)*

1. The Blue Bird Diner
2. Motor Haven
3. *Bachelor at Large*
4. Dizzy Dean
5. Larry Keating and Fred Clark
6. Bobby Buntrock
7. Lorelei Kilbourne
8. Joe Adams, played by John Vivyan
9. 1313 Mockingbird Lane, Mockingbird Heights
10. From left to right, Tige Andrews *(The Mod Squad)*, Adam West *(Batman)*, and Mark Goddard *(Lost in Space)*
11. Elsie Ethrington
12. David Brian
13. Camp Henderson; Vince Carter, played by Frank Sutton
14. They drowned while crossing the Snake River
15. Robert Rockwell
16. Alice Lon, Lawrence Welk's first network "Champagne Lady"
17. The Texas Rangers
18. Two minutes
19. Rhoda
20. Doctor
21. *The Goldbergs*; Eli Mintz played Uncle David
22. Jarrod, Nick, Heath (the bastard), Audra, and, in early episodes, Eugene
23. Box
24. Professor of Anthropology
25. One male subject with a problem was given advice by "the girls"

THE GAME GAME (page 76)

1. *To Tell the Truth*
2. *Dr. I.Q.*
3. *Jeopardy*
4. *Masquerade Party*
5. *Feather your Nest* or *Dream House*
6. *What in the World?*
7. *Beat the Clock*
8. *Queen for a Day* or *Strike It Rich*
9. *The Price Is Right*
10. *The $100,000 Big Surprise*
11. *Concentration*
12. *Jig Jag*
13. *Hollywood Squares* or *Tic Tac Dough*
14. *Brains and Brawn*
15. *The Sky's the Limit*
16. *Man In Your Life*
17. *Who Said That?*
18. *Mike Stokey's Pantomime Quiz*
19. *Let's Make a Deal*
20. *Tattletales*

FACE IT (page 84)

1. Jack Benny
2. Jim Nabors
3. Red Skelton
4. Don Porter
5. Allen Funt
6. Merv Griffin
7. Red Buttons
8. Walter Brennan
9. Arthur Godfrey
10. Bill Cullen
11. Bob Crane
12. Jon Gnagy
13. Peter Falk
14. Barry Livingston

AND NOW FOR THE $64,000 QUESTION (page 86)

"THE FUNNIES"

$64: Ham Fisher
$128: Lee Falk and Phil Davis
$256: J. R. Williams
$512: R. M. Brinkerhoff
$1,000: Mr. Julius Caesar Dithers
$2,000: Toonerville
$4,000: Uncle Elby and Napoleon
$8,000: 1. Major Hoople
 2. Martha
$16,000: 1. Castor Oyl
 2. Wimpy; the referee of the Tinearo-Popeye fight
 3. Elzie Crisler Segar
$32,000: 1. Uncle Bim
 2. Min and Andy Gump
 3. Chester Gump and Tilda
 4. Sydney Smith
$64,000: 1. James Swinnerton
 2. The San Francisco *Examiner*
 3. *Little Jimmy*

"GREAT BOOKS"

$64: *The Lost Weekend* by Charles Jackson
$128: *Life with Father* by Clarence Day
$256: *Not as a Stranger* by Morton Thompson
$512: *Tom Jones* by Henry Fielding
$1,000: Madame Defarge
$2,000: *Looking Backward: 2000–1887*
$4,000: Dostoevsky
$8,000: 1. Miguel de Cervantes
 2. Sancho Panza
 3. Part I in 1605; Part II in 1615
$16,000: 1. *The Jungle*
 2. *Dragon's Teeth*
$32,000: 1. A. B. Guthrie, Jr.
 2. 1950
 3. *The Big Sky*
$64,000: 1. *The Education of Henry Adams*
 2. 1907
 3. An historian

"MOVIES"

$64: *Summertime*
$128: *Johnny Belinda*
$256: *Goodbye, Mr. Chips*
$512: *The Good Earth*
$1,000: *The House on 92nd Street*
$2,000: *Road to Singapore*
$4,000: Katharine Hepburn, Cary Grant, and James Stewart
$8,000: *Little Miss Marker;* a "marker" is a pledge or security on a bet. Miss Temple was left as security on a bet.
$16,000: Mary Pickford
$32,000: David Wark Griffith
$64,000: Ford Sterling, Roscoe (Fatty) Arbuckle, Mack Swain, George Jesky, Hank Mann, Rube Miller, and Alfred St. John

"AMERICAN HISTORY"

$64: James Buchanan
$128: Thomas Jefferson
$256: Virginia, where eight Presidents were born.
$512: William Howard Taft
$1,000: San Salvador
$2,000: Mississippi, Florida, Alabama, Georgia, Louisiana, and Texas
$4,000: On October 18, 1867, during the administration of Andrew Johnson, Alaska was formally transferred from Russia to the United States
$8,000: The Union Pacific Railroad and the Central Pacific Railroad
$16,000: Oklahoma, New Mexico, and Arizona, respectively
$32,000: (Refer to an almanac or encyclopedia)
$64,000: John Adams, Thomas Jefferson, Martin Van Buren, John Tyler, Millard Fillmore, Andrew Johnson, Chester A. Arthur, Theodore Roosevelt, Calvin Coolidge, and Harry S. Truman

"ANIMALS"

$64: Roosters
$128: Bulls
$256: Ganders
$512: Drakes
$1,000: A cow, both are mammals
$2,000: The grampus, a sea animal something like a whale; and the potto, a West African animal sometimes called a sloth
$4,000: Ants and termites (which are *not* white ants)
$8,000: Every five to ten minutes, and not longer than an hour
$16,000: The Arctic tern
$32,000: 1. "Glutton" or Carcajou
 2. He sprays it with an evil-smelling glandular fluid
 3. The weasel family
$64,000: 1. The American bison, almost always called buffalo
 2. Sixty million, according to the American Museum of Natural History
 3. Twenty thousand

NOTE: These quizzes represent vintage *$64,000 Question* material and are, therefore, dated January, 1956.

THEY HAD A PAST (page 101)

1. Pinky Lee
2. Skip Homeier
3. Robert Stack
4. Lucille Ball

MISSING PERSONS (page 119)

1. John Beradino
2. John Gavin
3. Paul Hartman
4. Richard Long
5. Chad Everett
6. Carl Reiner
7. Patricia Breslin
8. Dennis Miller
9. Ray Bolger
10. William Windom

STAR SEARCH *(page 98)*

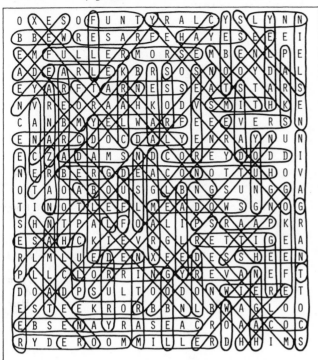

SERIES SEARCH *(page 122)*

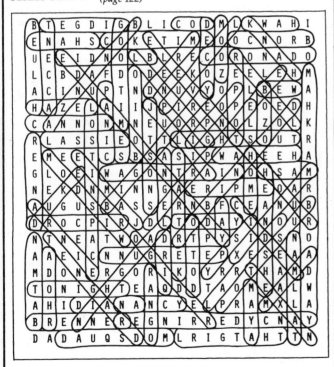

PROS, NOT CONS *(page 130)*

LAWYERS
1. Lee Majors
2. Texas
3. Gertie
4. Edmond O'Brien
5. Lawrence and Kenneth Preston

NURSES
1. a, *Medical Center*
2. b, *The Nurses*
3. d, *Emergency!*
4. c, *Marcus Welby, M.D.*
5. e, *The Edge of Night*

ENTERTAINERS
1. Eve Drake
2. The Copa Club
3. Century Studios
4. Gilliam and Norris Theatrical Agency
5. Dr. Brad Fairmont

NEWSPAPERMEN
1. b, *Ichabod and Me*
2. d, *Lou Grant*
3. a, *The Reporter*
4. e, *Big Town*
5. c, *The Debbie Reynolds Show*

TEACHERS
1. a, *Mr. Novak*
2. f, *Room 222*
3. b, *Lucas Tanner*
4. c, *Leave It to Beaver*
5. e, *Mr. Peepers*
6. d, *Our Miss Brooks*

DOCTORS
1. c, *General Hospital*
2. a, *Ben Casey*
3. f, *The New Temperature's Rising*
4. g, *The Doctors*
5. e, *Dr. Kildare*
6. b, *The Interns*
7. d, *Doctor's Hospital*

TREKKIE FEVER *(page 134)*

1. San Francisco Navy Yard
2. She was President of Desilu Productions, the original producers of *Star Trek*
3. George Samuel Kirk
4. Seventh
5. Spock
6. Command, Engineering, and Science and Ships Services
7. Sarek
8. "The Man Trap"
9. Five years
10. "Miri"
11. Pavel
12. Those resembling Earth's conditions
13. "Space, the final frontier . . ."
14. Lt. Uhura
15. "Cease and desist"
16. Thirteen
17. Harry Mudd
18. Captain Merik
19. A portable sensor, computer, and recorder
20. Lt. Commander Montgomery Scott

WHAT'S IN A NAME? *(page 138)*

1. Yvonne DeCarlo
2. Barbara Stanwyck
3. Don Adams
4. Jack Lord
5. Rock Hudson
6. Tony Curtis
7. Dorothy Collins
8. Danny Thomas
9. Barbara Britton
10. Ish Kabibble
11. Fannie Flagg
12. Janis Paige
13. Gale Storm
14. Jan Murray
15. George Montgomery
16. Robert Taylor
17. Gale Gordon
18. Red Buttons
19. Ray Milland
20. Craig Stevens

FUNNYGRAMS *(page 160)*

1. *Petticoat Junction*
2. *Heaven for Betsy*
3. *The Courtship of Eddie's Father*
4. *Mama*
5. *Alice*
6. *Mr. Peepers*
7. *Fair Exchange*
8. *Welcome Back, Kotter*
9. *Bachelor Father*
10. *The Danny Thomas Show*
11. *He and She*
12. *Those Whiting Girls*
13. *Professional Father*
14. *Car 54, Where Are You?*
15. *Good Times*

OUT OF THIS WORLD *(page 162)*

1. *The Outer Limits*
2. *Commando Cody*
3. David Vincent
4. O.S.O. (The Office of Strategic Operations)
5. Westport, Connecticut
6. Both played *The Invisible Man* in different TV versions
7. Sally Field
8. Tobor ("robot" spelled backwards)
9. The Time Tunnel
10. In an avalanche in Switzerland
11. Carl Kolchak
12. As a 1928 Porter automobile on *My Mother, the Car*
13. The Robinsons
14. Stranded on a desert island, Nelson picked up a bottle to spell out S.O.S. in the sand only to find that the bottle contained Jeannie
15. Rod Serling

BASED ON THE MOVIE *(page 164)*

1. Myrna Loy; *The Thin Man*
2. Hope Lange; *The Ghost and Mrs. Muir*
3. Raymond Massey; *Dr. Kildare*
4. Jack Lemmon; *The Odd Couple*
5. Joseph Cotten; *The Farmer's Daughter*
6. Blythe Danner; *Adam's Rib*
7. Ronny Howard; *The Courtship of Eddie's Father*
8. Ann Doran; *National Velvet*
9. Robert Sterling; *Topper*
10. David Niven; *Please Don't Eat the Daisies*
11. Johnny Washbrook; *My Friend Flicka*
12. Barbara Bel Geddes; *I Remember Mama*
13. Yul Brynner; *Anna and the King*
14. Leon Ames; *Father of the Bride*
15. Patricia Harty; *Blondie*
16. Christopher Connelly; *Paper Moon*
17. Wayne Rogers; *M*A*S*H*
18. Manuel Padilla, Jr.; *Tarzan*
19. Ralph Taeger; *Hondo*
20. David Carradine; *Shane*

About the Author

BART ANDREWS began his writing career in Mr. Siggins' sixth grade class when every student was asked to write a play. His entry, a parody of the popular *This Is Your Life* TV show, won first prize, a 25-cent ice cream soda. After that, there was two years' publishing and editing, with his friend Dick Niessen, *The Riverview News,* a small (3½" × 5") newspaper in upstate New York. "Everything was going along great until we published the obituary of a guy who hadn't died," Andrews recalls. "But we met every deadline, which is a lot more than I do today!" Then came New York University where he studied to be an English teacher, and then, lo and behold, an offer to write comedy in Hollywood. Since then, he has written television shows, nightclub acts, TV commercials, songs, and books (eleven of them). He's a likeable chap, worries about his weight, drives a red car with a license plate that reads "I LV LCY," and collects back-issues of, yes, *TV Guide.* In other words, he's a hopeless TV addict, but proud of it.